LET THE
WIND
CARRY ME

Gill Terry Causey

LET THE WIND CARRY ME

How Curiosity Can Open Doors of Perception and Learning

LET THE WIND CARRY ME, LLC | Los Angeles, CA

Published by

Let the Wind Carry Me, LLC | Los Angeles, CA

Publisher's Cataloging-in-Publication Data
Causey, Gill Terry.

Let the wind carry me : how curiosity can open doors of perception and learning / Gill Terry Causey. – Los Angeles, CA : Let the Wind Carry Me, LLC, 2020.

p. ; cm.

ISBN13: 978-0-9601057-0-0

1. Causey, Gill Terry. 2. Sailors--United States--Biography. 3. Voyages and travels. 4. Ocean travel. 5. Sailing. I. Title.

G477.C38 2020
910.45--dc23 2020914813

Second Printing

Project coordination by Jenkins Group, Inc. | www.BookPublishing.com

Front cover photograph © Benson Lee

Cover design by John Barnett
Interior design by Yvonne Fetig Roehler

Printed in Korea
25 24 23 22 21 • 5 4 3 2 1

This book is dedicated to my dad for introducing me to the ocean world.

To my mom, who was always the contrarian, a very independent spirit who gave me support to be the individual I am.

To my sister, Nancy, and my best friend, Rick, for teaching me to fear no one and always to have a sense of humor.

To Nancy Griffith, for introducing me to the world of blue water.

To Alan Olson, for drawing me into the world of building the Matthew Turner *ship.*

To my family and friends and sailing buddies, for being involved in my life and the world of sailing.

To Steve and Cheryl Kornberg, for all the blue water sailing experiences they included me on, especially working as an escort boat with the Polynesian Voyaging Society.

To my friends and family, who always supported and cheered me on in my sailing adventures.

CONTENTS

"You are adopted too."

Chapter 1

MY BEGINNINGS

When my parents told me I was adopted, my initial reaction may surprise you, but immediately I said, "It figures." I was born in Los Angeles in 1950 to a biological family whom I never knew, and my adoptive parents finally told me when I was in the seventh grade. I will never forget that day when the subject of adoption came up in class at school, while this kid was sharing how he was adopted. After arriving home from school that day, I was telling my mom all about it, when she said, "We have something to tell you. You are adopted, too."

Family and Friends

It turns out my sister was adopted three and a half years earlier, but at that point, it all made sense to me because we were all such different people. We didn't look alike or have any similar personality traits. You could say that I took the news quite well because my parents were really good people.

You may be thinking that I immediately started the process of tracking down my biological parents, but, frankly, I had no interest in doing that. Of course, I thought about them from time to time, but there was no motivation for me to find them. Besides, I wouldn't have anything in common with my biological parents other than my DNA.

I did go through Ancestry.com and 23andme.com and found out that I am 75% Swiss and 25% Ashkenazi Jew. Ashkenazi Jews are individuals who built religiously based communities in Central and Eastern Europe, and they are known for using Yiddish, a German language written in the Hebrew alphabet.

It was interesting to be contacted by third or fourth cousins and to find out that one was a Holocaust survivor who traced my biological family back to 1528.

Gill and June Causey

My adopted mom's side was all Swiss, and her father's side was German and Italian. I also found out that my grandmother and great aunt were Swiss. There is a lot more of my family history that is still a mystery, but I am really not that curious about it.

I understand people who have been adopted may want to know more information about health history for concern of medical issues, while others find it is not always that rewarding to search for their biological parents and family. My adoptive parents were such wonderful people who were conservative, tolerant people, but I had no interest in hurting them in any way by searching for my biological family. I had a great family and was surrounded by loving parents who took great care of my sister and me.

When I was taking care of my mom, the caregiver had mentioned that my mom had talked about my sister. Her biological mother had been married to a military man and got pregnant with my sister, but I never knew or heard any story about my biological parents, any siblings, or extended family. What kind of relationship would we have? I had enough family around me and certainly didn't need any more. My dad had two brothers, my uncles, so I had three cousins whom I was very close to. My grandmother on my dad's side was a Southern woman who cooked amazing Sunday dinners of fried chicken, mashed potatoes, and green beans.

My mom's stepfather, my grandfather, left Ireland when he was 16 years old and became a merchant marine before ending up as an engineer on a trade boat in China. My adoptive father traced his family all the way back to Jamestown; they had come across the ocean from Holland or England in 1607, becoming one of the oldest families in the United States, even before those who arrived on the *Mayflower*.

During 1953–1954, I developed polio. When we were staying in our Balboa Island house, after our visit to the Fun Zone amusement park, I collapsed on the floor. Paralysis set in, and I was bedridden for almost a year. Luckily, my parents were proactive and had a nurse come in every day to help me with bathing and to exercise my muscles, the Sister Kenny method. As a result, those preventative measures kept me from having any long-term effects.

There were other friends I knew who were struck with polio and ended up with a shorter leg or arm and paralysis around the eye. Fortunately, I did not end up with any of those side effects. However, it was quite confining being bedridden for so long because both my sister and I were basically quarantined for seven months, something she held against me for a long time.

Even though my sister and I were quarantined, my parents could leave the house to run errands and so on, and, of course, my dad still went to work. He graduated from Stanford as an economist, and his dad, my grandfather, was a building contractor in Nashville, Tennessee, where they were originally from. Eventually, they moved to Palo Alto, California, when he was a teenager, and then as a young man out of college, he moved into a bachelor pad in North Hollywood.

> "I developed polio and was bedridden for a year."

He became partners with one of the guys he lived with, Frank Rhodes, who was from Alabama. They built a building/development business after meeting a guy who needed to construct a group of medical buildings. In fact, they built the first high-rise apartment building on Wilshire, a medical center in Crenshaw, and they continued to build and established an office for their business in Glendale, California.

My parents wanted me to go to college, so I chose a Quaker school known as Whittier College and became a conscientious objector.

A conscientious objector is a person who has claimed the right to refuse to execute or carry out military service on the grounds of freedom of thought, conscience, or religion.

Quakers were also known historically as "friends," a Christian group that used a formal name of Friends Church or the Religious Society of Friends. The Quaker movements are generally united by their belief that each person has God within them. In the mid-eighteenth century, formal legislation was granted to excuse or release objectors from fighting in the military.

When I was 10 years old, I was inspired by the book *All Men Are Brothers* by Albert Schweitzer, which had been given to me by the deacons in my Presbyterian school. Presbyterians have a strong background of believing in the brotherhood of man and the idea of nonviolence and that you shouldn't kill people. *All Men Are Brothers* is an incredible book about the life of Schweitzer, a Nobel Peace Prize winner, who had the guts to live his dream and strive toward all of his aspirations. He was an expert organ player and philosopher, he wrote books, and, then, in his thirties, he decided to completely change direction by studying to become a doctor.

Traveling to Gabon in Africa, and starting from scratch, he set up a hospital that was so desperately needed in that area. He was an unbelievable man, and his book is littered with philosophy and insight into truth, humanity, and righteousness. An amazing soul, he lived to about 90 and was extremely active right up until his last day on earth.

Before graduating from Whittier, I had started out as a math major, but my counselor turned out to be a fascist during the Vietnam War in 1968. It was a tumultuous time with a lot going on, and since I couldn't stand my counselor, I started looking into other subjects. I ended up liking the political science counselor Ben Burnett and decided on history with a dual major that included taking some law classes. In fact, I considered going to law school, but by the time I graduated and took the exam, I realized it wasn't in my future.

After graduation, I joined the labor union and became a laborer. I worked for about six years before moving to Hawaii. For about five years, I had been living in Laguna Beach, California, one of Southern California's premier coastal destinations. Known for its artist colony, it is one of Orange County's hidden gems, located halfway between San Diego and Los Angeles.

My parents had saved up an insurance annuity for me, which gave me about $40,000, enough to buy a little house in Laguna Beach. Early on, I had been very impressed with the beatniks and the Bohemian scene, enjoying the freedom of Laguna within the artist community, and I decided that was where I wanted to live. Since I wasn't earning enough money to get a mortgage, I found the cheapest house available—only 600 square feet on a corner lot.

For two years, I held on to that house before selling it to buy a little duplex on a 35 × 45-foot lot and then fixing up the lower unit and renting out the upper unit. It was during a time of inflation, and in eight months, I was able to sell it and double my money. Immediately, I bought another place and fixed that up, as well as one more house after five years. It was an old shingled place with a studio unit that I rented out to a young friend, Candy.

Unfortunately, Laguna was becoming too crowded, and it was getting much harder to get around, so I decided to take some time off and took a trip to Costa Rica with my friend Mark Carmichael. We were gone for 10 months and drove all the way through southern Mexico that borders Guatemala, then into

El Salvador, through a portion of Honduras, into Nicaragua, and then crossed the border into Costa Rica. We intended to continue but we ended up getting kidnapped in Limon, Costa Rica. At the time, we were planning to go on to South America, but the kidnappers had something else in mind—mainly to get money from us.

It all happened when I was trying to get some cashier's checks, but the bank hadn't been open that day. Some local guys were standing nearby and suggested that we go back behind the bar that was close by. Since there were three of us, I figured we would be OK, but I kept having bad feelings about it. My friend wanted to buy some marijuana from these guys, but they turned on us quickly, acting like they were the police, and they started beating us up.

They had me drive to the bar, where they took my two friends and held them at gunpoint. Meanwhile, I was negotiating with them to find a way to pay them off and get out of there. One of them looked at me and said, "We want $500 and your camera."

"I will give you $700 if I can keep my camera," I quickly replied. I couldn't believe how spunky and demanding I was, considering the seriousness of the situation, but I wasn't going to put up with anything less to get my friends out of our predicament. Fortunately, I was able to negotiate with the kidnappers and managed to get us all out of there alive.

> "My whole plan changed."

Driving in my truck, we ended up going to the west side of Costa Rica to stay there for a while and explore the area since my plan was to sell my house in Laguna and move to Costa Rica. We were heading north to the US, about two hours south of Oaxaca, when I heard a big bang on the side of my truck. Immediately, I thought it was my tire, and I pulled over at the next pullout. My friend, Betty stayed in the truck while her boyfriend, Rory, and I got out to check out the damage, when, all of a sudden, a couple of banditos jumped out of the bushes and started poking me in the chest with a knife. I started bleeding all over, and since I knew Spanish pretty well, I started yelling at them to stop.

It occurred to me that they were going to throw us over the cliff. Since I had cash with me, I pulled some out of my pocket and threw it on the ground at their feet. When they looked down, it gave me a chance to jump in the truck and get away. We drove to a truck inspection station and went inside for help. At that point, I was covered in blood because I realized he had also jammed a knife into my back when I had turned around. It looked rather rusty, and I explained to the attendant that I needed a tetanus shot and some antibiotics.

The attendant looked at me horrified, then immediately called for a nurse, who took good care of me. They wanted me to stick around to tell the police all that had happened to us, but immediately I said, "No, that's OK. Thank you." I had no interest in going through the Mexican legal system, so I thanked them again and left.

By the time I arrived home in Laguna, my whole plan had changed. I was 25 years old at the time and quickly realized that I didn't want to live in a foreign country. My sister had moved to Hawaii in 1974, and I recalled how much I loved the islands when my parents took us there on vacation.

I flew to Hawaii and stayed with my sister long enough to find an acre and a half in a rural section of south Kona. After visiting my sister, I flew back to Costa Rica to let go of the house we were renting, picked up my friend, and started organizing my plan to move from the ever-growing Laguna to Hawaii, which I did in 1977.

I had made a trip to Alaska in 1973 through the Yukon and national parks, but I quickly realized that even though it was beautiful, I had no desire to live in a place that was so cold, especially during the wintertime. Having been to Hawaii several times, I found I loved the people, as well as wearing shorts all the time and going barefoot. Living in Hawaii turned out to be a blessing. Initially, I bought a place for $130,000 with an interest rate of 10% and put down $30,000, but I soon realized that I was not a farmer and didn't want to spend my time picking nuts.

A while later, I found a tiny place that was all one room on a hill overlooking the channel between the Big Island and Maui, so I sold the house and moved there. About a year later, the people I had sold the house to called me and said, "We're sorry. We can't afford this house any longer," and they moved out even though they had already put $30,000 down. I sold it again, this time to someone else who also had it for one year and simply gave it back to me, so I ended up getting that house back twice.

In Hawaii I was surrounded by water, but for the first time in my life, I was not able to go out on the water. I had always been into fishing, and I did manage to go out with an albacore fisherman who let me sleep on his boat from time to time. It was at that moment when I realized that I wanted to be on the water for the rest of my life. I was determined to find a way to do just that. I saw an advertisement for a celestial navigation class to be held at a local marine store and decided to take the class; there I met a woman named Nancy Griffith, and we became good friends. She was doing charters for the Oceanic Society, and I started helping her.

Eventually, we decided to buy a boat together—an iron-riveted sailboat that was 56 feet long—and we converted it so we could do charters. Immediately, we received a contract at the University of Hawaii and proceeded to travel from Honolulu to Kauai, Molokai, Maui, Lanai, and the Big Island. In the meantime, I went through a month-long course to get my captain's license and had enough sea time to meet the requirements. I had to have at least 720 days of sea time to start with, considered as 24-hour days working at port or at sea.

> "We decided to buy a boat together."

Since I had been on boats most of my life, I had accumulated plenty of sea time, already. Plus, I had to take the marine course for being a captain and start at a 100-ton license with sail endorsements and, later on, increase that to all oceans with radar endorsement.

For about 20 years, we ran the boat commercially out of Kona, Hawaii. That included trips down to Christmas Island, where the government had hired us to bring its parliamentary ministers back to the island, which had an airport. At Washington Island there is no harbor; someone came out in a little boat to welcome us but then needed gas to get back to the island. We ended up taking on 11 people because they didn't get many chances to get off the island, and it was too hard for us to refuse them. We made a lot of trips down to the island nation of Kiribati, Washington Island, Fanning Island, and Christmas Island, advertising that we would pick up and deliver. It didn't matter where we needed to go because we just loved sailing so much.

On one trip, we took scientists from Tahiti to Pitcairn, picked up another group, and brought them back to the Tahiti island. It was a wonderful experience because we were greeted so kindly at this small rock of an island. The people spoke a seventeenth-century Old English mixed in with the Tahitian language. When we arrived, they divided all of us up to spend the night in individual homes, where we met Irma and Ben Christian, relatives of Fletcher Christian.

The channel between the big island and Maui is 16,000 feet deep, with water funneling through at a rapid pace. It is one of the most formidable places to sail, and I have had people crying on the boat because they were so worried about crossing that channel. When we worked with the university, we would not sail upwind in gale warnings, but we would sail downwind. In fact, those conditions were stated in our agreement, and we were paid $500 a day for lay days and $700 for actually running the boat.

I learned a lot about those difficult conditions—they can be quite challenging. I've noticed that people who come from the Southern California coast are quite nervous about sailing conditions having to deal with difficult anchoring in remote bays and small harbors with limited facilities, making it quite challenging to navigate the waters. After a while, you learn which areas to go to and anchor in.

I met Nancy not long after her husband died, and though we didn't have any kind of romantic relationship, we enjoyed each other's company and were thrilled to be able to go sailing. I started sailing with her on a 42-foot wooden ketch that leaked a lot from the top. On our first sail from Kona to Kauai, it was about a 48-hour sail that took us through all sorts of storms and squalls, but it was wonderful to sail through the Hawaiian Island chain.

It was quite an experience, sailing around the interisland waters prepares you for sailing the sea. The boat was called the *Nelly Bly*, named after a young lady in the 1920s who was a newspaper reporter and decided to do an around-the-world trip so she could write about it for the *New York Times*. She circumnavigated the world while writing these stories and was an independent, adventurous young woman, and that is why that was such a great name for Nancy's boat.

We got caught in a storm one time with 10- to 12-foot swells that forced us to seal off the hatchway so the water wouldn't gush below deck. I ended up with a storm jib, and we were still moving along at 6–7 knots, but when a swell would come, we had to sail down it and be very careful. In those conditions, you have to stay alert, but with a small sail up forward, it gave us a leading edge that helped out the helmsman with a little jib up, giving us plenty of sail under those conditions. It prevented us from rounding up and rolling over.

> *"Sailing around the inland waters prepares you for sailing the sea."*

I didn't really lay out a focused plan or route to make a career of working on the water, but I took advantage of every opportunity I had to be at sea. When the opportunities showed up, I was always very grateful for them, which led me to sailing. My partner was friends with an attorney, Steve Kornberg, who was quite good at what he did with California real estate; he distinguished himself there with landlord/tenant cases and subsequently got licensed in Hawaii.

Molokai Music Festival crew

He soloed to Hawaii and loved sailing just as much as we did. He was one of the original partners in the sailboat that Nancy and I bought. When we got the contract with Blue Marine, we had three captains: me, Steve, and Nancy. We took turns being captain and became good friends through the process.

When I used to do Holo Holo, a non-charter a few times a year around Molokai, Steve would come along as we started going into the Pacific. By the way, holo holo means "Let's go" in Hawaiian. Locals use it as a term to go do something active. If you say, "We go holo holo," it means "Let's go cruising!" By itself, holo means "to sail."

Eventually, he got a 50-foot steel boat, and we would sail that together, taking turns crewing. It didn't matter what kind of sailboat we had access to; we both felt fortunate to be successful enough to enjoy the world of sailing.

"holo holo"

"Let's go cruising!"

Lauren (my mom's caretaker) and my best friend, Akamai, with me at the helm

"I traveled to Cartagena."

Chapter 2

THE ADVENTURE BEGINS

At the ripe old age of 28, I traveled to Cartagena, Columbia, with a good friend of mine, Mark Bowers, before moving on to Ecuador, Peru, and Bolivia. There were 20 of us that traveled on the back of a Mercedes truck, and every night, two of us would take turns going to the market to prepare three meals a day at the site where we camped out in tents.

VANS

My nephew, Eric, and his family and friends who all traveled to Peru in 2018. This was one of the trips where I wanted my family and friends to see a place that I thought was so amazing.

We also managed to get to Bogota, Columbia, known for its colonial architecture, picturesque restaurants, and museums. Since it was holy week, I was able to see many of the well-preserved churches located throughout the historic area, and I was transported back in time to an era when Spain controlled that prosperous territory. Most of the churches were built during the colonial period, and the designs of the altars, paintings, and sculptures were extraordinary.

In Bogota, we stayed at a hotel where all the drug lords hung out. We met an emerald dealer who had a shop out near the mines. He sent his driver to pick us up and took us to his shop, where there was a guy standing at the entrance with a machine gun. When we went inside, a nice lady offered us scotch and coffee as he laid out little packets of emeralds.

"That is how you buy them," he said, educating us about emeralds. We were fascinated with these gemstones and learned about their brilliance, color, and cut. Of course, we had to buy some, and though there were dangers being where we were, I never had any fear. I was cautious but soon realized that our hotel was the headquarters for buyers and sellers to meet, so the emerald dealers would hang out there to find customers.

At this point in my story, you might be thinking that I took too many chances in my travels around the world so far. Though I found myself to be shy at times, my folks had always made me feel comfortable with traveling anywhere from a very young age. I never felt intimidated or was afraid to go places, and I have always been fascinated with South America. It was an incredible way to see that part of the world, plus we were with a group, not just wandering around by ourselves.

Montserrat is a mountain that is over 10,000 feet tall and rises above the center of old Bogota. Climbing Montserrat began as a pilgrimage to the Sanctuary of Montserrat, where religious visitors go to worship, but you can also see an incredible view of Bogota from up there.

People were crawling on their hands and knees and using cardboard to climb Montserrat mountain in order to get to the white church to perform their penance or atonement at the nunnery. It is a 1500-step hike, and considering that you are starting at over 8500 feet in elevation, it is an extremely difficult climb. Even though I had grown up around many people strong in the Catholic faith, I had never seen anything like that before or experienced such religious penance. We stayed and watched them practice amazing sacrifices, and it was evident that they were very serious about their beliefs.

Cruising down the Amazon

From Bogota, we flew to Quito to rejoin the group, after having stayed behind. We took a bus to the Ecuadorian Amazon and then took a truck to the tributaries, where we began our hike. We traveled on boats to a tributary in the Amazon before hiking in the jungle for about three days to stay with an Auca Indian tribe that lived in the Amazon forest. There are actually almost 500 indigenous tribes in the Amazon rainforest, with 50 of them that have never been exposed to the outside world. They have their own social life, and the kids never go to school, only learn from the elders in the group.

We found it funny that every evening they would round up all their animals—dogs, goats, etc.—and gather them all together in a shack warehouse. All night, all we could hear was a grumbling noise coming from that shack, knowing full well they didn't want to be together in such an enclosed place. Of course, they would let them out in the morning, but we soon realized that this was done to protect the animals. We all had to be careful and watch every step we took because there were snakes everywhere.

One of the most common freshwater fish found in the Amazon basin is the piranha. We actually enjoyed it grilled over an open fire, and it was delicious. Most of the piranha we caught were about 6–8 inches in length, but they can extend up to 24 inches in rare cases. Known for their razor-sharp teeth, insatiable appetite, threatening look, and fearsome reputation, they come in all sorts of colors, from yellow to black, from dark red to steel gray with colorful underbellies. Since they are in most of the rivers in the Amazon, you have to make sure you don't have any cuts on your legs; you have to be bleeding only a little bit for them to attack.

We also had to be careful of the Fer-de-lance snake, known in Spanish as *Barba amarilla*, which means "yellow chin." It is an extremely venomous snake that can be deadly. We were trudging through mud in humid, moist areas and had to watch out for them everywhere we stepped. These snakes have a poisonous venom that can quickly destroy your flesh.

While visiting that Indian village, our main diet was monkey meat and roots. The roots were quite tasty, almost like a potato, but the monkey meat was a bit chewy, though flavorful. At least it kept us full. These tribes are used to living off the land and shooting blowpipes to kill monkeys, which they then skin and roast over open fires. They also eat toucans and peccary pigs, as well as plants and herbs foraged in the forest. Their lifestyle has caused many of them to have flat feet, which actually helps them climb the trees to kill the monkeys.

In the early morning hours, one of the tribal members woke me up and wanted to trade: his blowpipe—a quiver that he made with tipped arrows, where local cotton is used for stuffing—for my towel. The blowpipe was about 6 feet long in order to blow these tipped arrows to kill the monkeys with a nerve poison, curare, that paralyzes the animal. Since I was going back to where there were plenty of towels, I told him, "I don't want your blowpipe because it is too big and bulky for me to carry."

He looked at me smiling, "Trade?"

I loved how it was made and went on to say I wouldn't take his blowpipe but I would trade my cotton towel for the quiver with the arrows that came in a little basket, about the size of a golf ball. It was made of cotton-like material to put in the pipe before they blew it to create pressure so that it would send the arrow farther into the trees.

Our guide had made arrangements for us to stay in the communal lodge that had walls and a roof with one large platform where we laid out our sleeping bags. We interacted with the Indians as much as we could by using sign language. Since I spoke Spanish, I was grateful that some of them spoke that language. Their ears were elongated, made possible through rings with holes in them, and their faces were tattooed with different colors. Most just wore loin cloths, and the women were bare breasted, but they were very kind to us, and meeting all of them was quite the experience.

We stayed with the tribe for three days before hiking out. Later, after traveling by truck, we arrived in Cusco, Peru, a nice change from the Amazon forest as we wandered through the open-air markets. We bought cocoa leaves and chewed them with lime, something that helped us deal with the altitude. Small bits of the cocoa leaves are used in tea known as mate de coca, which also helped with altitude, as we were 10,000–11,000 feet up. The tea helped with my breathing by opening up my airways and served as a mild stimulant that really helped me deal with the altitude.

Potatoes are quite popular in Peru and are used in hundreds of recipes that include chicken and alpaca (llama) meat. In the Andes of Peru, alpaca meat is an important food source that is low in fat and cholesterol, with less calories than lamb, beef, or pork. One of the more popular dishes is known as *causa*, a recipe made with potatoes,

Reserva Nacional Pacaya Samria in the Amazon Peruvian National Park

VANS

Cruising down the Amazon in Peru with my nephew's family

vegetables, and seafood. There is a wonderful fishing fleet that runs up and down the coast, so that gives them plenty of access to lots of seafood.

We were there for about two weeks and traveled to the upper plateau of Lake Titicaca, where there is a floating village of people who live on reed mats that sit on the lake. It is the highest navigational lake in the world, so it is a little surreal to be on a boat higher than most of the land masses. The villages are on top of these floating islands where the Indians live, and we were fortunate to be able to spend some time with them.

From there, we went to La Paz, Bolivia, about 42 miles southeast of Lake Titicaca and surrounded by the high mountains of Altiplano. It was so high up that when cars drove by, we couldn't even hear them. It was a very different world. Unfortunately, I started to suffer from altitude sickness, something that was unusual for me, because I had been dealing with it for the past month. As a result, my friend and I decided to leave the trip and flew on Bolivian Airlines to Santiago, Chile.

At that time, I was vaguely aware of the Latin American politics that had been going on in that area for almost a decade. It appeared that the farmers of this green strip of land, wedged between the Pacific Ocean and the Andes Mountains, had resisted the construction of a copper mine they said would pollute the water and destroy their livelihoods. They felt betrayed by Chile's president after the government gave the go-ahead to build Southern Copper Corporation's Tia Maria project. They didn't like the fact that the president was giving priority to a multinational company and did not want to accept it. The copper mines were operated by American companies, but the president wanted to socialize the country and take the copper mines away from the American companies.

Salvador Allende was a popular president elected by the people, but the head of the military, General Pinoche, didn't like what he was doing. He was deposed and eventually killed. However, copper is a very valuable material and needed to be protected. Copper accounts for 60% of Chile's total exports and is the main driver of the South American nation's economy. Chile looked like a peaceful island, but the angry farmers' unrest could not be ignored.

When we landed in Santiago, Chile, we learned that people who were protesting were being rounded up and killed in the stadiums. It was quite a frightening period in history, during which many people would disappear and be killed. We were the only Americans on our airplane, and when we walked into the airport, five guys in trench coats immediately grabbed us and interviewed us for hours on end.

Both of us could speak Spanish, but that didn't seem to matter as they searched through all of our bags. They thought we were smugglers, but we were young and acted goofy, making jokes about the whole situation. Eventually, these henchmen got tired of dealing with us and let us go. When I look back on our circumstances at the time, I realize that we were so lucky to get out of there alive. Many people continued to disappear, and though we were wary of this, we weren't guilty of doing anything wrong.

Once we got through that interrogation, we wandered through the main city, where I found a tailor who made me a vicuna coat. The vicuna is a South American member of the camel family closely related to the alpaca, llama, and guanaco. The vicuna, the smallest

> "They thought we were smugglers ..."

of the llama family, lives in the higher altitudes and is covered with a remarkable long, fine, soft, and lustrous coat that varies in color from a pale white to a light cinnamon brown, with long white fleece hanging from the base of the neck to the lower flanks.

The fibers are quite strong, are resilient to the elements, and are used to make high-priced coats, shawls, and dressing gowns. Their hair is used like that of goats, but they are now a protected species. I kept that coat for a long time and eventually gave it to my nephew's wife. I will always have fond memories of the people of Chile who were wonderful to us, as they really are more refined European-like folks.

After spending about two weeks in Chile, we then flew on to Buenos Aires in Argentina. We were there for about a week and then went to Uruguay. With a climate similar to that of the French Riviera, the area is a socialized small country that has been in existence since the 1920s with an established government that has created a lot of wealthy people. If you ever get a chance to go to Buenos Aires, you must see the incredibly beautiful casinos with massive domes made of stained glass that sit on the top of the buildings. They truly are a sight to see in a recreational city. Uruguay is a ranching country and is run by ranch plantations, much like a small Texas.

When we flew into Buenos Aires, we discovered that our hotel was having an international conference, as all the Latin American presidents were converging and meeting on the premises. When it was time for us to leave our hotel to go to the airport, the streets were so clogged with traffic that we couldn't get a taxi. We were complaining about our situation near the doorway when a very nice driver came up to us and said, "I am the Peruvian president's driver and would be happy to take you to the airport."

He told us he knew the president was in a conference for quite some time so he would be off duty for a while. He explained that traffic would stop to let us go by and didn't charge us for the trip! He said he was happy to do it since he found us to be quite likable. It was a very gracious and hospitable thing that he did for us, and we were so grateful that he took the time to get us to the airport on time. On the way home through Brazil, we stopped in Rio de Janeiro before heading back to the US.

After flying back to the states, I then moved to Hawaii. I had already sold my house in Laguna, and by late 1977, I was in Hawaii on an acre and a third filled with about 20 macadamia nut trees. Since I had no desire to become a farmer, I hired my neighbor to pick the nuts, and he stored them in 100-pound bags. I paid $5 per bag and sold them to the co-op for $45 per bag, providing me an income of about $1,100 a year.

It wasn't a lot of money, but at least I was making something from all those trees. It took a lot of time and effort to take care of those trees because they have to be trimmed and fertilized in order for them to produce more macadamia nuts. However, I didn't want to get into all of that; I simply wanted more freedom to do what I wanted to do.

During that time, I wasn't able to get out on the water as much as I did when I was a young boy with a 14-foot Boston whaler. Here I was in Hawaii, surrounded by water without any means to enjoy it. There was an ad in the local paper for a course on celestial navigation for sailing that a woman named Nancy Griffith had posted. She was a three-time circumnavigator (meaning she sailed around the world three times), and I responded to her ad right away. First, I took her course in navigation, and later she offered six two-hour lessons on her 42-foot boat, *Nelly Bly*.

Nancy Griffith at the helm

ORACLE
Fly Emirates
OMEGA
CAMPER

America's Cup in September of 2013

That was the moment when I fell in love with blue water sailing, a world that suited me perfectly. As a kid, I suffered with asthma and allergies and was even in the hospital a few times, so breathing was an issue for me. Going out on the water, where the air is so clean and fresh, always made me feel so good when experiencing the wind and the beauty of nature.

When I met Nancy, I realized that I could do this type of traveling as an adventure. Before, I was always traveling in some sort of vehicle, but being on a beautiful boat on the ocean—there is nothing better. It is like a romance that you have, falling in love with the adventure and allure of the sea. In books about sailing, authors often talked about the reality of the boat world, which included always shifting, moving, and living in a deprived environment that could take away the romance of it all. But it never did that to me.

Though I remember a time sailing in New Zealand when it was bitter cold, I still enjoyed the experience and was just happy to be on the water. Being in the tropics, always barefoot and in swimming trunks, I enjoyed that lifestyle, too, and I actually prefer it.

Since 2013, I have been taking my nephews and families on trips to New Zealand and French Polynesia, and we even stayed on Marlon Brando's island, an eco-friendly resort. When Marlon began filming the movie *Mutiny on the Bounty*, he fell in love with Tahiti and purchased a 12-island atoll named Tetiaroa and developed the land so he could explore the benefits of eco-conscious living while turning it into an environmental-friendly resort.

All of these amazing trips have been made possible with my good luck in the real estate industry. Since my dad was an economist and my mom an accountant, they had an incredibly positive influence on me, especially when it came to the real estate business. I quickly learned that the charter business is also a great business if you want to live that kind of life, but you won't make much money in it.

When my mom passed away, I took over the family business, and having grown up in it, I was very comfortable with any dealings. That is why I always stayed in the real estate world. After all, I had to find a way to pay for all those trips.

Sunset Sail crew with my mom, June

Chapter 3

ON THE WATER

After having crewed with Nancy on a 42-foot boat, I decided that it was time for me to get my own sailboat. During the process of searching for a sailboat to purchase, I came across the boat that appeared in the Elvis Presley movie *Blue Hawaii*. It was for sale, at a price of $44,000. Since I wasn't in a hurry and was taking my time, I started the negotiation process in July, and by October 1983, I had talked the sellers down to $22,000.

Hokule'a

Double-hulled canoe Hokulea

I was ready to bite the bullet and move forward with the purchase when Nancy asked me, "Would you like to buy a boat together?"

Without any hesitation, I said yes. It was such a great offer to be a partner with someone of her experience. She had come across a 56-foot riveted iron sailboat through one of her sailing students. It had been built by the German navy for sea cadet training before being captured off the coast of Scotland during World War II, so it had quite a history.

Eventually, it was auctioned off in Australia where two young Australian brothers took on the daunting task of putting her back together, something that took seven years to accomplish. They managed to get a sponsor—Douwe Egbert tobacco, which allows users to Dutch roll their own tobacco. The product comes in a blue tin, an image of which was proudly displayed on the big blue sails during their first voyage, with the slogan, "The satisfaction of doing it yourself."

By the time the brothers arrived in Hawaii, they were ready to sell it. One brother was married with one small child, and the other brother was a bachelor. We were able to purchase the boat, and though we had some partners that were involved in the purchase of the boat, Nancy and I were the main owners. In fact, Nancy had already planned for us to make money with this boat. Our first contract was with the University of Hawaii to handle its Blue Water Marine Lab program, which involved our planning sails throughout the ports in the state.

Nancy and Terry sailing on the Goodewind

We started working with the boat at Snug Harbor in Honolulu for the fall session. Meanwhile, I managed to get my captain's license and took the boat on her first operation out of Oahu, known as the Heart of Hawaii. We then ran her for a couple of weeks out of Port Allen, picking up school kids while running a morning charter from 8 to 11 a.m. and then one from noon to 3 p.m., week after week until the end of the semester.

Sea Cadets Hawaii arriving at the Coast Guard Base in Honolulu

In the spring, we took her back to Oahu, Molokai, Maui, Lanai, and the Big Island. I loved it because I was getting a lot of experience docking the boat and working with the students. In fact, that is when I realized how much I enjoyed teaching as well as having the opportunity to expose these students to sailing. Conducting scientific studies, the students collected algae and performed a deep-water study that included lowering a pipe with a spring closure as deep as possible. They placed a Styrofoam cup inside the pipe, and when they brought it up, it was one-third the size, which showed how the pressure affected the cup.

We had a davit for the quarter-inch wire run by a hydraulic pump installed on the boat that we ran off our engine. A davit is a crane-like device used on ships for raising, lowering, and supporting equipment such as boats and anchors. Sometimes the term refers to structural arms in other applications such as a suspended load used in the navy or used as a man-overboard safety device to retrieve people from the water.

We would also throw overboard a huge benthos net that was about the length of the boat, and we dragged it along the bottom. When we pulled it up and placed it on the deck, we analyzed all that was brought up and found all sorts of interesting things. We continued to sail along the Waianae coast, working off of Oahu Island, which spans 17 miles along the western coast of Oahu.

After that we worked out of Snug Harbor for the fall session. Later we did a trip to Kauai, working off of the Napali Coast, which is a sacred place, defined by its extraordinary beauty of emerald green cliffs with defined ridges that tower over the Pacific Ocean. The beaches are gorgeous with stunning waterfalls that plummet to a lush valley below. For centuries, Hawaiian settlements flourished in these narrow valleys, existing only on the fish they could catch and the food they could grow.

If you ever get a chance, I highly recommend that you explore the Napali Coast by sea for the best views, or perhaps you might enjoy the remote beaches or hidden sea caves. The natural beauty will leave a deep impression on your heart and soul—at least it did for me.

We also sailed by the Molokai Mountains, which make up the island of Molokai. They are quite impressive with their multiple deep gorges, thanks to the thousands of years of erosion. Unlike other mountain ranges, Molokai is shaped like a foot, due to a huge landslide that occurred 300,000 years ago. You can find amazing marine fossils at the base of the volcano; scientists discovered that these fossils were deposited there by a massive tsunami thousands of years ago.

As it turned out, Nancy's friend Marty Vitousek served as our main contact for communications through a single sideband radio while we sailed. His dad had been the speaker of the house in 1941 when Pearl Harbor was bombed, and he and his dad were flying their prop airplane and had to figure out another place to land to avoid the zeros.

Between the fall and spring sessions, our next sail was scheduled in November to Christmas Island, my first blue water voyage of about 1,000 miles. It took 10 days to get there, and since the route was all downwind, it was an easy sail. However, sailing back was a different story because we were sailing against the wind.

Fanning Island friends, 1980s

We happened to take Marty's ex-wife, Anne, who was hearty as hell and planning to go to a smaller island close by, but we needed to check in with customs first at Christmas Island before going to Fanning Island. She was very knowledgeable about the area because she was stationed there during the war.

In between my work for the University of Hawaii and this cruise, the government hired us to pick up the parliamentary ministers and bring them back to Christmas Island before flying them to Parliament. A parliamentarian is a consultant whose primary goal is to study, teach, promote, and disseminate the principles and rules of parliamentary procedures, as found in Robert's Rules of Order. Contracting with a parliamentarian usually entails portal-to-portal travel expenses and time necessary to review governing documents in an organization.

The crew of the Goodewind

We agreed to pick up the parliamentary ministers in exchange for some drums of diesel fuel because the whole trip took about a month and a half going from Christmas Island to Washington first and then crossing some incredible currents and winds that were hard to deal with at times. It is much harder to go east than it is to go west.

We were supposed to just pick up the parliamentary minister, but it turned out that no one had been to the island for quite a while, so we ended up taking 11 people instead of just one from Washington to Fanning Island. Some stayed there while we went on to Christmas Island. That was my first experience sailing blue water.

We went back to do the spring session sailing out to all of the islands, working with different island schools from fifth grade to junior college level. After that, we received a contract with the University of Cambridge to take its scientists to Pitcairn Island out of Tahiti.

In the meantime, I met this guy named Bruno as well as one of the schoolteachers, Maria, and her husband, Henny, who pleaded with me to take Bruno when we left Fanning. Actually, he had jumped ship, and the government was going to take him to jail. At the time, I wasn't the captain of the boat; it was actually another friend, Steve,

> "That was my first experience sailing blue water."

as well as Nancy, though we all took turns being captain. It was our second trip, and at the time, Steve was the captain, so I had to let him make the decision.

He said to me, "We have to talk to Nancy."

"Absolutely not" was Nancy's immediate response.

We brought Bruno anyway, and he turned out to be a charming Frenchman, showing up at the boat with bread pans and a sextant. His real name was Bruno Delala, and he became a lifelong friend to us all. Eventually, he married a local girl, and he now lives on Fanning, running a guest house for surfers and visitors.

When we got the contract with the University of Cambridge, Nancy wanted me to deliver the boat to Papeete in Tahiti. Nancy had been involved in a sailing freighter company doing freight work, but I was a little worried about going into a French port because I had heard how awfully the French can treat Americans.

I said to Bruno with a smile, "You have to come with me and protect me since you are French."

Bruno agreed and came along to help me deliver the boat. Fortunately, we had a mooring where we could leave the boat after we checked in with the officials. It was a beautiful morning when we arrived in Papeete, anchored, then tied the boat to the wharf so we could go meet the officials with our paperwork. They were gracious and quite charming, so all those rumors I had heard were totally untrue. I had never met nicer people and was delighted and thrilled to be treated so well.

We agreed that Bruno was going to stay with the boat and then Nancy would come so we could do the first trip from Papeete, Tahiti, to Pitcairn Island, as the sail was a considerable distance. When I went down to do the second voyage, I had a good crew with a lot of sailing friends who worked hard to get the boat ready. We installed a weathervane and took the boat over to the main harbor in Tahiti to start getting provisions and meet with the scientists.

Dear family and close friends, Tetiaroa, French Polynesia

The problem for me was we had quite a trip ahead of us and we didn't have any wind. We were fortunate to have wind during the first 24 hours of the trip, but then we had to motor the boat for six days. In the Gambier Islands, Mangareva, Rikitea, is the largest village on the island, known for having a mad priest in the late 1800s who forced the people to work the land and build a cathedral that was made out of coral and mother of pearl. Mangareva is the central and largest island of the Gambier Islands in French Polynesia, surrounded by smaller islands Taravaiin to the southwest and Aukena and Akamaru in the southeast, plus islands to the north.

Mangareva has an extraordinarily high ridge that runs the length of the island with a large lagoon that spans 15 miles. It contains all sorts of fish and shellfish that helped the ancient islanders survive much more successfully than on the other nearby islands without reefs. Mangareva is an important travel link to Pitcairn Island because the only way a traveler can reach the island is to fly to Tahiti, then to Mangareva. From there, it is a 32-hour boat ride to get to the island. Some people can reach the island by a commercial ship, but

> **"We were met by the islanders who actually lived where the mutiny on the *Bounty* occurred in 1789."**

that is happening less and less because the ships do not pass close to Pitcairn Island.

We were taking four scientists and four crew, but as we headed out, we realized we were running low on fuel, so we made arrangements with a guy on Mangareva to get more fuel. We managed to take on some extra drums of fuel and lashed them to the decks, and off we went to Pitcairn Island. We were met by the islanders who actually lived where the mutiny on the *Bounty* occurred in 1789. They were lovely people who greeted us kindly and told us where to anchor.

The island is only a mile long, but the people have lived there for hundreds of years. They sailed there with the *Bounty* ship, then stripped and sunk her. The story goes that the mutiny on the Royal Navy vessel HMS *Bounty* occurred in the south Pacific on April 28, 1789. Disgruntled crewmen, led by Lt. Fletcher Christian, seized control of the ship from their captain, William Bligh, and set him and 18 loyalists adrift in the ship's open launch. Bligh was an excellent navigator and sailed all the way through the Fiji Islands, about 1,200 miles to Tamora, with a very simple compass and open boat. Only one man died out of 16, and those mutineers settled on Tahiti and Pitcairn Island.

Meanwhile, Captain Bligh traveled over 3,500 nautical miles with a goal to reach safety and begin the laborious process of bringing the mutineers to justice. The relationships between Bligh and his crew deteriorated after he started handing out harsh punishments and abuse. Eventually, Bligh was forced from the ship while 25 men remained on board. No action was taken against John Adams, one mutineer, as descendants lived on Pitcairn into the twenty-first century.

After the mutineers arrived, they knew about Pitcairn, but it was misplaced on the English charts, with the thought that the English would have a hard time finding them since it was mis-charted. There were some Tahitian men and women who stripped the boat and burned it. By the time the first visitors came, about 17 years later, the only remaining mutineer was John Adams.

Up at the school, they have the old ship's bell in Adams Town, and the locals still speak the language, a kind of Old English, seventeenth-century dialect mixed in with Tahitian. It is quite interesting to hear those odd phrases such as "Arrgh!" They sound so different from British English.

Descendants of Fletcher Christian welcomed us with all the other families and treated us to a party feast before dividing us up to stay in different homes on the island.

We left four scientists there, but we had four scientists to take back to Tahiti. When we took them into Mangareva, the police were not around. It was my job to get a special permit because we were sailing past Fangataufa and Mururoa Islands, where nuclear testing had been done. They were very cautious about anyone passing by those areas, though the island was only six miles long and six miles wide.

It has a lagoon area of about 17 square miles. We caught a lovely tuna there. The scientists wouldn't eat it, but tuna is pelagic, meaning it migrates, and it was probably just passing through. We love fish so much, and since it wasn't glowing, we figured it was OK to eat.

When we landed at Rikitea, normally I would have to check in with the armed guards, but no one was there, so I left a note for them saying that we would check in with them on the way back. When we arrived back, they weren't very happy with us, but since I did come back and left them a note, at least they knew I was honest with them.

When leaving Mangareva, we had about 1,100 miles to sail in order to get to Tahiti. The wind blew like hell, and I had to be really careful with the crew because I certainly didn't want the boat to tip over sideways or capsize. The only sail I had up was a storm jib that pulled the boat forward. Normally, I would have the main sail up, but that would have pulled the boat more side to side. It was a little harrowing, to say the least. We had two people on watch who would monitor the winds, watch for any potential problems, and take action if needed.

That was when I was used to sleeping for only a couple of hours at a time before having to get up to check on things. I am used to it now, but I still managed to get into a deep REM sleep, even on a boat—because you never know how much sleep you will get or for how long. Even with my lack of sleep, I found my experience with the University of Cambridge to be quite interesting, to say the least.

Goodewind *anchored at Mokuaniki between Maui and Molokai in the Pailolo Channel*

Next, I formed a crew and was ready to sail north. At the time, my friend Quentin's neighbor in Pahoa had a son who was 14 years old and always getting into trouble. I told him that he could be part of the crew on the *Goodewind* (the name of the boat—after a German pirate who was quite revered). He ran the full gauntlet saving his crew after his head was chopped off.

Anyway, I told the father, "If you can get Josh down to Moorea, about nine miles from the island of Tahiti, I will take him with me."

Josh agreed to come, showed up on time, and turned out to be a wonderful young man as well as a great friend who did a lot of sailing with us. Eventually, young Josh got the hang of it and became a good sailor.

There were three of us who were going to sail *Goodewind* 2,700 miles from Tahiti—a good distance, especially since there isn't much out there. It was going to take us two to three weeks, and we had a lot of squalling in the Convergence Zone, an area to sail that can last up to three days.

Many sailors, both novice and experienced, fear storms as the greatest danger on the water, even though more emergencies and fatalities can occur during times of relative calm waters. The Convergence Zone, known by sailors as "the doldrums" or "the calms" because of its monotonous, windless weather, is an area where the northeast and southeast trade winds converge.

Sailing north, we had a lot of squalls, which were quite terrifying and could last 15 minutes or an hour. We had to be extremely careful because we could capsize, the sails could rip, or we could get dismasted. I had a steering vein that would steer the boat when a squall hit and the winds changed. It was like a mini cyclone with a circular force of power and a direction that is typically in the Convergence Zone. There would be a squall and then no wind. We had to use some of the wind to get out of the squall without getting the brunt of the dangerous winds. In other words, we were able to skirt the sides of it to stay safe. The wind vein seemed to handle it quite well, and the boat would veer off, making the passage less dangerous.

I put everyone on a single three-hour watch schedule. Of course, everyone is available if you need help, but, basically, each crew member would be on watch for three hours and then be off for nine hours. That gave us a chance to get to know each other, make food, and enjoy the trip.

That was when I fell in love with French Polynesia, especially the croissants. The island had its own little bakery, and every morning, we enjoyed fresh baguettes with canned New Zealand butter, which is delicious. Plus, we could take it with us on the boat because it didn't need to be refrigerated. We would scoop it out and spread it on French bread—pure heaven.

Jacob and Meralda Warren, on Pitcairn Island, were descendants of the mutiny on the *Bounty*, and Meralda had written a cookbook that included a recipe for sweetened biscuits. On the return to Tahiti, I took on the task of making those biscuits, which were a great treat on the way back. They were crispy on the outside, moist on the inside, and delicious with jam. Since we didn't have refrigeration, anything like that was a luxury. We had a condenser on the boat, but it made so much noise rattling the boat and gave everyone a headache, so we didn't bother using it.

We still managed to eat well and in an ice cooler packed New Zealand legs of lamb and frozen chicken, which would last about a week so we could enjoy some good meals. In addition, cheeses sealed in their packages and meats like ham were foods that we could carry for a long period of time because they didn't need refrigeration. After those food items were gone, we hoped to catch fish.

Fortunately, we caught a 75- to 100-pound tuna and cooked parts of it in a pressure cooker. We left it pressurized until we were ready to use it, then pulled it out and mixed it with onions and mayonnaise to make tuna salad on fresh-baked bread from the oven. I had found a recipe in a James Beard cookbook, *Menus for Entertaining*, that suited us on the boat. All you have to do is mix the flour and let it rise for an hour. Here is the recipe:

4-Ingredient French Bread

Prep time: 15 minutes
Cook time: 45 minutes
Yield: 2 loaves

Ingredients:

2 cups of whole-wheat flour

2 cups of white flour

1 tablespoon of kosher sea salt

2 packages of active dry yeast

1 teaspoon of sugar

1½ cups of lukewarm water

Directions:

1. Dissolve the yeast into the warm water and stir in the salt and sugar. Add the whole-wheat flour, a cup at a time and then mix in the white flour to make a smooth dough using a wooden spoon.
2. Form into a ball and cover it and let it rise for an hour or two.
3. Divide into two French style loaves. We used a baking pan or you can put the loaves on a cookie sheet. Sprinkle with cornmeal if you want. Let it rise for 5 minutes.
4. Place in a cold oven and turn it up to 400 degrees and bake for 40 minutes.

***

Since we didn't have to preheat the oven, that helped keep the boat cool. For a really crunchy loaf, allow the loaf to cool for 30 minutes on the rack of a partially open (and off) oven. Remove and let cool a bit. In an hour, we would have fresh-baked, crusty bread. It was a nice way to do it because while the oven was heating up, it would bake the bread. It is a great recipe.

Through it all, I have completed hundreds of Interisland sails, including 12 sails to French Polynesia, 11 sails to the Line Islands, 7 sails around New Zealand, 3 sails to Australia, 5 sails to Fiji, and one sail each to the Cook Islands and the Solomon Islands. A lot of those sails were done on the boat of Steve Kornberg, who had been a partner and then a captain on the *Goodewind.*

We became long-time friends, and when we sailed on his smaller boat, I kept him from falling overboard. He was holding on to some rail that failed, and I managed to throw him a line. We have been friends ever since, and he sailed with me on the Line Islands (Kiribati) trips before I started crewing for him around New Zealand, Australia, and Mantegna Island, New Caledonia, and Solomon Islands.

"Steve and I were hired by the Polynesian Voyaging Society."

Chapter 4

SAILING IN THE ISLANDS

Steve and I were hired by the Polynesian Voyaging Society to escort *Hokulea*, the Hawaiian term for the star Arcturas, on his 50-foot steel boat, the *Gershon II*.

GERSHON II

The Gershon II, *Steve and Cheryl Kornberg's boat, which I sailed on for many years around the Pacific—Cook Islands, New Zealand, Fiji, Vanuatu, Solomon Islands, and Australia*

Today, Polynesia is a group of nations that were colonized independently. The boundaries of the original Polynesia nation stretched from Aotearoa, New Zealand, in the southwest corner, to the Hawaiian Islands in the north, to Rapa Nui (Easter Island) off the coast of South America. Spanning over six million square miles of open ocean and islands, the Polynesian Triangle is still considered one of the largest countries found on the planet today.

Over the course of a thousand years, the Polynesians have built vessels and used currents to populate the offshore islands. They sailed double-hulled canoes for thousands of miles to the east as their skills in wayfaring and navigation grew. It is fascinating to learn how they sailed the open seas in these dugout canoes. The stars in the sky were used to navigate everything around them using the wave patterns and currents to determine which direction to head. Take a look at the following diagram to see how the Polynesians divided the sky into quadrants. When a star rises at a specific point on the horizon, it will ultimately set in the opposite quadrant from where it originally rose.

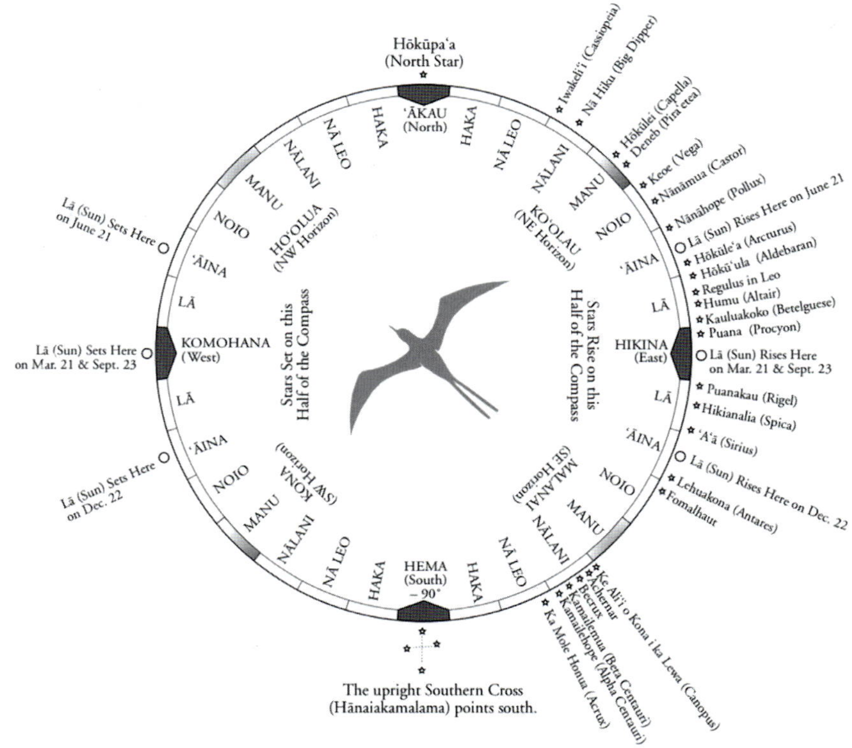

Hawaiian Wayfinding Compass (downloaded from tourmani.com)

For example, if the sun is rising in *hikina* (the east), sailing out in the middle of the ocean, navigators can tell at every sunrise which direction is east. Similarly, at every sunset, navigators knows that where the sun crosses the horizon is *komohana*, or west. Sailors don't have to wait until sunset to know which direction is west, since the moment they saw the sun rise in the east, they can instantly discern which direction is west by looking 180° behind them. From these two directions sailors can then discern north as well as other points on the compass and keep the canoe on the desired heading to reach their destination.

Hokulea, May 2015, Polynesia Voyaging Society

However, it takes more than the sun to keep a proper heading, and Polynesian navigators used this same technique with dozens of different stars. Throughout the night, navigators can watch a procession of stars as they appear on the eastern horizon and correlate from their location which direction the canoe is facing and heading. In theory, the process is simple enough, once you are able to recognize the stars, but the constellations change with the boat's latitude in proximity to the equator. Navigators know to adjust for these changes and can also accommodate for unforeseen challenges such as clouds or stormy skies.

In addition to the stars, navigators will also use currents and wave patterns to change their direction and heading. Feeling the rhythmic movement of the boat, rather than looking at the waves, navigators can tell the direction from which a swell is rocking the boat. Since ocean swells follow seasonal patterns, navigators can use the rocking of the boat to determine the heading and direction of the boat in either daytime or cloudy skies. It has been said that master Polynesian navigators could close their eyes and discern five different swells all gently rocking the boat, simply from a change in movement if their heading had drifted off course.

Me with two Maori dancers in New Zealand

Traditional New Zealand canoe, May 2015

Back in 1976, the Polynesians were not using an escort boat, and many boats ended up flipping, floating for hours in the wind until they could be rescued. When Hokulea was on a trip, this happened with Eddy Aikau onboard, a well-known Hawaiian surfer and lifeguard who was part of the crew. Since he had a surfboard on board, he took off and paddled to the west end of Molokai to get help. Unfortunately, he disappeared, and we never found him. From that point on, the Polynesian society and Nainoa Thompson, who was the head of it, determined that they would never send the double-hulled canoes out without an escort boat. Safety became their top priority.

As a result, Steve was hired to escort them during their practice runs and to Oahu and Kahoolawe islands. From a historical standpoint, after the attack on Pearl Harbor in 1941, the United States declared martial law in Hawaii. Kahoolawe, a place considered sacred to native Hawaiians, was transformed into a bombing range. Weapons testing started almost immediately with ship-to-shore bombardment and, later, with American submarines testing torpedoes by firing them at shoreline cliffs.

Over the decades, the wars changed, but bombing continued. In 1965, the infamous "Sailor Hat" tests were conducted on the island: three tests of 500 tons of TNT were detonated to simulate the blast effects of nuclear weapons on shipboard weapon systems. It was heartbreaking to everyone, especially to native Hawaiians.

Eventually, the head of the US Navy offered to end the bombing practice and give the island back to the Hawaiians. The Protect Kahoolawe Ohana also sued the navy, and a few years later, the bombing was ordered to stop. In 1993, Congress voted to end all military use of Kahoolawe and transferred the island back to the state. After decades of bombing, Kahoolawe was wounded, littered with debris and unexploded weaponry.

Today, about 25 percent of the island is still uncleared. Despite the dangerous conditions, thousands of volunteers continue to go to the island to help in the healing process. Although it's a job that will take generations to fulfill, hope still remains with every step, every tree planted, every stone that's lifted. It is all part of the process of healing the island.

Hokulea, *Tasman Crossing, May 2015*

It was commemorated with a ceremony on the beach in Maui, facing Kahoolawe, that included several Hawaiian officials and representatives from many organizations. They had woven a coconut fiber rope that almost 100 people held from one end to the other as part of ceremony during the dedication. When it was time to leave, we went back to Smuggler's Cove, where there are wooden military barracks and up on top of Kahoolawe is a Heiau (Hawaiian Temple) made of rock walls where the Hawaiians were going to have a special blessing.. We were honored to attend the ceremony, but we stayed on the boat in Smuggler's Cove.

This was when I started working with Steve and the Hawaiians escorting boats throughout the inner islands. There was a big event scheduled by the Hawaiians and those from Maui and New Zealand, as well as locals from Polynesian Cook Islands, to converge in Tahiti for the big day. New Zealand had one canoe, Cook Islands had two, and the Hawaiians had three, but all had escort boats.

We were to escort them from Hawaii to Tahiti and then to Marquesas Island and then back to Hawaii, which is about 3,000 nautical miles. The place where we went in was Nuka Hiva, a port on the main island, before eventually escorting them back to Hawaii. That was a three-and-a-half-month escort. I did that with my *Goodewind* boat and escorted the *Makali'i* canoe which means "eyes of the chief" in Hawaiian mythology and is also the name of the constellation, Pleiades in Greek mythology, known as the 7 Sisters. Steve escorted the *Hokulea* canoe, while Alex, a Russian boat builder, escorted Hawaii *Loa*.

When all the canoes arrived at Marquesas Island, all the people were lined up along the beach before we got in our dinghies to come ashore. They were so warm and gracious, welcoming us to the island by putting leis around our necks. There was a huge table of incredible food to feast on. In fact, they fed us every day for five days. It was so magical to be surrounded by the beauty, music, singing, and warmth of the people welcoming us to the island.

Escorting the canoes was our job, as long as it was a double-hulled canoe, which was actually a 50-foot catamaran, but they preferred to call them double-hulled canoes instead. As long as they could sail, we just followed using traditional navigation. Mind you, they had a GPS locked away in a box for safety reasons in case of trouble, but, basically, Makali'i (which means "eyes of the chief") is the Hawaiian name for the Pleiades star cluster, also known as the Seven Sisters, and can be found in the constellation Taurus.

In the fall, the appearance of this star cluster at sunset marks the beginning of the Harvest Festival, known as Makahiki. It is the time of year to celebrate the end of the harvest, when battles and wars ceased and sporting games began. The word makahiki means "year," and the Hawaiian year is measured from the rising of the Makali'i star group in the eastern horizon that begins in mid-November.

A healthy harvest means survival, the celebrations of the Makahiki and the symbolism of a new year that represent new beginnings. The beauty of the canoe is that it allows each person to find his or her own path, to seek specific roles and responsibilities that fit that individual. The canoe is a reflection of community that combines the strength and talents of those individuals seeking to share those gifts throughout the Hawaiian Islands. The captain was Clay Bertelmann, and Shorty Berelmann, his brother, was the navigator.

Back in the '70s, I met Shorty Bertelmann and his co-navigator Chad Baybayan, who were wondering whether they were fully prepared for a long ocean voyage. In addition to memorizing star patterns and nautical charts, they had to watch the weather daily as they made decisions in response to the weather at sea.

In 1975, the older brother of Clay Bertelmann first saw Hokulea when it sailed into Kawaihae Harbor while he was helping to rebuild the walls of Pu'u Kohola Heiau. Clay sailed from Hawaii to Tahiti and learned navigation well enough to become captain. The greatest challenge of any sea voyage is to stay awake in order to keep track of the course of the canoe and the ever-changing weather. He actually learned to take short catnaps for about three to four minutes, which allowed him to regain his concentration.

On the voyage to Tahiti in 1985, he was grateful to spot a school of dolphins that lived in that area of the ocean. The sighting confirmed his faith and trust in the ancient tradition of navigation that Mau Pialag represented. Eventually, Shorty and Clay built a 54-foot canoe, Makali'i, to serve the Big Island. It was launched in 1995 under a double rainbow, a sign of a blessing from the gods, as Hawaiians looked at Makali'i as the "eye of the chief."

We navigated toward the Marquesas Islands, one of the most remote groups of islands in the world, northeast of Tahiti, then through Tuamotus, a chain of atoll islands that runs all the way to the higher islands of Gambier, where Mangareva is located. With the exception of Motu One, all the islands of the Marquesas are of volcanic origin. Basically, a volcano erupts from the ocean and builds up lava until it bursts through the ocean and continues to rise higher and higher until it forms a viable island.

> "Healthy coral reefs are some of the most valuable ecosystems on earth."

A reef system develops around the island, and, eventually, the volcanic cone of the island erodes. Sometimes, all that is left is the reef and some land mass that is very flat. Some of the old islands have been worn down to reef and land mass about five feet above the surface of the ocean. Usually, they are covered with palm trees and, because of the volcano, develop a porous surface of the land. Tubes are formed that collect fresh water, creating an aquifer.

Healthy coral reefs are some of the most valuable ecosystems on earth, providing food, jobs, coastal protection, recreational opportunities, and other services to billions of people throughout the world. Unfortunately, many coral reefs have been damaged or destroyed because climate change, human impact, and other factors.

Even though corals look like rock, they are actually living animals that can be destroyed or hurt by careless snorkelers. If you ever get a chance to visit the islands, make sure that you don't walk on, stand on, or touch coral, as this can kill the living coral polyps that build the structure of the reef. Wearing sunscreen that has damaging chemicals can also damage coral, so many sunscreen lotions have been banned in Hawaii.

Of course, you never want to break off a piece of coral, either. Be aware that places where you rent snorkeling equipment sell fish food, but you don't want to feed the fish because this will upset the natural balance of the reef and can create more aggressive species in that environment.

My big trip in 1995 was to escort *Makalii* for three and a half months from Hilo, Hawaii, to Tahiti, Marquesas, and back. We spent about a week in Tahiti and five days in Marquesas. The rest of the time, we were at sea. Recently, I watched a documentary about Tracy Edwards, who dreamed of racing a sailboat around the world. In the '80s, open-ocean sailboat racing was a male-dominated sport, so she was only able to sign on as a cook for an all-male team for the 1985–1986 Whitbread Round the World Race, an exhausting and demanding 33,000-mile undertaking.

In 1989, she put together an all-female crew to enter that race, something that was unthinkable to most men in the yacht-racing world. She received so much criticism, anger, and disapproval because everyone told her that she and the crew would die. That didn't stop these women, who restored an old racing yacht christened Maiden, in which they finished the nine-month race second in their class. Back then, it was a first to see women working in a shipyard, and all the guys had brand-new boats, so they didn't have to do much work on them at all. Many of the men would sit in the local café and watch the women put their boat together.

The great thing about that building process is that they learned everything they needed to know about their boat because they installed and put every single item and piece of equipment needed on that boat themselves. They did the rigging, all the electronics, the navigation station, even the plumbing, so when they put the Maiden in the water, they knew that boat from the inside out.

It brought tears to my eyes as I watched that documentary again because I could feel all those emotions they were experiencing. Sailing the open ocean is challenging, exhilarating, exhausting, and adventurous all at the same time. Though they came in second in their class overall, the best result for a British boat since 1977, their ship doctor said, "There is a bigger picture here, and the bigger picture is what we have achieved."

On our sails in open water, we always had at least two people on watch, sometimes three, with four-hour watches that would rotate day after day. At night, it was so beautiful because we could see the stars clear as a bell. You start to get very comfortable seeing the constellations at night with their rise and fall and what position they are in during the night. In other words, you become very familiar with your night sky and how and where the boat is headed, and that creates a very secure feeling that you are always headed in the right direction.

While the ladies on the *Maiden* were experienced, they had very good technicians who plotted their course for the best speed and conditions, lower on a high or sailing between different situations in the weather. It all depends on the course you decide to take, which can determine whether you are ahead of a boat or not.

For example, the concept of going fast-forward in a lift, or pinching in a header, has been around for as long as I can remember. Referred to as "making a bearing gain," this is when you sit on the rail and watch as you make "trees" on your competition. Trees are equal to boat lengths. You have to understand how to sail high and slow or low and fast. It is important to be aware of what you are doing when you are going for a bearing gain because you don't want your boat to spear off into a corner, potentially sailing farther for a shift that never happens. When sailing in the open ocean, you have to monitor what is happening around you. The crew needs to be aware of the changes and notify the helmspeople as to what is working for you and your boat.

You have to have good helmspeople and maintain a good course. You don't want to weave or fall off one way and come back. In other words, you may need to keep your course more straight rather than deviated. It also means maintaining the amount of sail up that you need for the winds you have, so as the winds pick up, you might want to reduce the sail for safety and comfort for a more efficient ride, and then the boat will respond. As the winds diminish, you want to put up more sail.

When it comes to racing boats, you have to be aware of the amount of weight on board because that will determine how fast your boat can go. On the *Maiden*, the women weighed less than the male crews, and they were limited to bringing one bag only with essential items.

While racing is exciting, I am known as a cruiser, not a competitor. In our line of sailing work, we were just trying to get people from place to place. I filled up my storage area with tons of food, cookies, and canned peanuts so we always had good food on board. Plus, I had a water maker with storage tanks, and that made it nice to always have fresh water. The race boats probably have water tanks too, but they rely on dehydrated foods for lighter weight. Too much weighted canned food can diminish your speed on a sailboat.

When sailing, I enjoy the process of harnessing the raw power of nature, the weather, and the wind to keep my sailboat moving. Doing so is based on technique and knowledge that run much deeper than operating a powerboat. There is such a rich history in sailing, but most of all, I enjoy spending time with family and friends on board. Unlike other activities on the water, sailing requires complete cooperation among the crew. Sails have to be tweaked, winches need to be turned, lines need to be trimmed, and we all work together to keep the sailboat moving in the right direction through weather, wind, sunshine, and rain.

I was very successful in operating good passages, not overburdening people with too many tasks, traveling as light as possible. My sailboat was a heavily displaced boat of riveted iron, not aluminum or fiberglass, so we were quite stable, and it would just drive through the water. Most of my passages would last anywhere from two to three weeks.

Weather was something we always kept an eye on, and, occasionally, a front would come through, often rather quickly. In New Zealand, we had a front that came over us that lasted 24 hours, and then it was gone. Sometimes, they can last longer, but you hope that you don't get caught up in any cyclonic conditions. On the edge of one is not so bad, but if you are right in the middle of the path, there are some strategies to employ such as dragging something heavy behind you to keep you from going down the swells too fast. There is a risk that you can pitch forward, something you don't want, and, therefore, you need to slow down that momentum. You also don't want to go sideways, so you have to keep the sails in position.

After the storm, we ran into a couple of computer scientists who told us they had locked themselves in their boat and stayed below until the storm passed, but that can't be very comfortable.

I would rather be out there in the elements trying to do some kind of maneuver. You want to try to get out of the way of a storm or weather system as soon as you realize it is out there.

When we escorted the canoes to Marquesas, there were about seven or eight canoes. It turns out Marquesas is known for a big fly that bites and is rather obnoxious, but we never ran into them. Even so, the Hawaiian authorities asked us to check all of our luggage 70 miles away from shore and spray our entire boats to make sure we weren't going to bring this fly from Marquesas and introduce it to Hawaii. Not one person ever saw a fly, and there was never any evidence of these pests. It was a bit frustrating because we had been at sea for so long and had to sit out there for days before they gave us permission to land and come ashore.

Sailing the Goodewind, *Kealakekua Bay,*
where Captain Cook first landed the Endeavor

This had never happened to us on all my other comings and goings. As the captain, I always could get off the boat and go into the harbor while the officials would clear our passports, something I have done many times. This would happen mostly on the Kona side, but I have made it into Hilo, and the check-in process is much smoother.

On one occasion, I was on the *Goodewind*, Steve was on *Gershon II*, and Alex was on the third escort boat, *Kama Hele*, out of Hawaii. There was another escort boat with the tail ready, the double-hulled canoe from New Zealand, two out of Cook Islands, and two out of Tahiti. As they started to leave, the officials declared the French cruising double-hulled canoes unsafe; though they were beautifully designed, they were not safe to do an ocean voyage, so they had to drop out. They prevented them from participating because they were not seaworthy enough to do the trip to Marquesas and Hawaii.

It's hard to give a subjective opinion based on design, weight, etc., but that can certainly affect their decision. They looked a bit narrow, and most catamarans are wide, but their center of gravity was lower. The narrow canoes could be pushed over in the ocean and therefore are not considered safe.

Everyone believes that their boat can do anything, and you depend on it. We had a very sturdy, ocean-proven, ocean-going boat that could handle 50 knots of wind easily. When you go out on the ocean, there are two things you rely on: a good, strong boat that will get you out there and back and a good crew to work the boat. That is what gives you the confidence that you can go anywhere. We always had a great crew and a strong boat and knew the boat could go wherever we wanted. It was built by Germans, who are known for being rather precise and excellent ship builders.

Sometimes, if I had a new crew, I would take them on an inner-island sail to see how they would do. One of the routes we would take is one of the most formidable channels to cross in the world because

An aerial photo of Tetiaroa Island, where my family and I visited last year. It is a good example of the atoll islands that I used to sail in French Polynesia, off of Tahiti.

This is the island that Marlon Brando owned.

it runs 16,000 feet deep, with a volcano on one side (Haleakala at 10,000 feet high) and the Mauna Kea land mass of 13,000 feet on the other side. The trade winds would pop through there, which is like compressing flowing air through a narrow slot, so it accelerates and intensifies. It is called a Venturi effect (Spanish for "narrow pass").

Trade winds are the permanent east-to-west prevailing winds that flow in the Earth's equator area, blowing predominantly from the northeast in the Northern Hemisphere and from the southeast in the Southern Hemisphere. Between the seas and the winds being pushed between Maui and the islands, it would make for steep waves and swells with intensified winds. It is not unusual to get 25–30-knot winds crossing that channel, but it can gust up to 50 knots. Trade winds have been used by captains to sail ships across the world's oceans for centuries.

Some people thought it was the worst crossing ever because the boat would flex so much. In fact, people were so scared that they cried, terrified we would capsize because the waves were quite formidable. I would try to calm them by saying, "I have made the trip a hundred times. Plus, we have an iron boat that is strong and low-profile and built for this kind of weather and sailing."

Even though I tried to reassure them, I would often put them behind the wheel so they could feel like they had some control. I would teach them how the boat handles bad weather and redirect their anxiety into something useful so they weren't just sitting there worrying about things going wrong. They would be actively involved in the boat, but they never expected to see such big seas and the boat sliding down these swells. It was very dramatic, but when you know the boat can handle it, have good crew to run the boat, and have done it a few times, you understand that this is survivable. You have to have confidence in the boat as well as the crew.

One time we were towing a canoe on the windward side of Maui through the Pailolo Channel to the Kaunanakai main port on Molokai. Just as we started going down the channel, our steering cable broke, and we had to do the repair right then. The canoe took off, and we yelled, "We'll join you later!"

We had a new steering system with a round half-circle that has a cable running through it and sits over the rudder post that goes to your rudder. Around that you have pulleys and a steering wheel, like a bicycle chain that is attached to twisted wire, and that runs down the post to pulleys that translate and turn the wire. It will run around twice your quadrant so when you turn the wheel, it turns this half circle of bronze that will turn your rudder.

It has broken twice, and both times, I had to climb underneath to put on a spare cable, but it only takes about 15 minutes to fix. Eventually, I had an 11-foot tiller made for the boat that I could put on top of the rudder post so it would allow me to sit on the front of the cabin while the cable was being repaired. We always had backup systems and spares—you have to. When you are out at sea, you have to be able to make repairs when needed. You can't expect to sail across an ocean without experiencing some breakages or problems with your equipment or sailboat. Knowing how to fix and repair them is key to keep on keeping on.

*"We sailed from Kona
to the Line Islands."*

Chapter 5

LIFE IN POLYNESIA

Seven sails with Steve and his wife, Cheryl, on *Gershon II* around New Zealand and three sails into Australia, New Caledonia (an overseas territory made up of a main island and several smaller islands in the region of Melanesia in the southwest Pacific Ocean), and Fiji, which included five sails, were all amazing sailing trips. In 1991, we also sailed from Kona to the Line Islands (along the equator), where we rescued Bruno yet again. He managed to get to Washington Island and was married to a woman named Tabita, but then they got food poisoning. They had a huge feast for their wedding, but when they took off on their boat, they both experienced food poisoning.

When they left Washington Island or Terranea, which it is called in the Gilbertese language, there was a young boy who had come from 2,500 miles away in Gilbert, the capital city, Tarawa of the islands. At eight or nine years old, no one knew whom he belonged to, so Bruno and Tabita decided to take care of him. After their wedding ceremony, together they sailed off that island but soon encountered a strong current, the counter equatorial current, which ended up drawing them back to the same island. Unfortunately, their whole boat broke up into pieces on the reef of the shore, and they were stranded.

We sailed from Fanning to Washington, where Steve dropped us off to help him move his stuff back. There is an inland freshwater lake that used to be run by an English coconut plantation. Workers would pick loads of coconuts from the shoreline to dry in the sun and then collect the coconut meat, known as copra. It would be shipped and sold for processing into coconut oil.

On a side note, mature coconut meat is from coconuts that have been left on the tree longer. It is thicker and very oily and typically dried to make products such as coconut flakes and chips. If it is further processed, it can be made into cream, oil, and coconut milk. This was done by an old English company years ago before the islands were bought, mainly Fanning and Washington Islands.

When we arrived in the inland lake, we were in awe of its beauty. Later, we went back to the village to one of the houses near the village. They hosted a meal for us, and as it turned out, they served canned corned beef on homemade coconut bread, an island favorite. It was delicious. We managed to get one of the communal long boats from one of the churches where we were to load Bruno and Tabita into this little boat. We took them to the beach that sloped down into the ocean where the boat had to glide through the reefs.

Fortunately, on this boat they had an outboard engine that could be raised up, so we all climbed into this boat, and the whole village started to shove the boat down a slope to the ocean to get us into the water. The boatman lowered the engine into the water, started it, and got us through the reefs. We picked up the *Gershon II* and eventually arrived in Fanning Island, about 80 miles away, but we had to tack, a sailing maneuver that turns the bow toward the wind so that the direction from which the wind blows changes from one side to the other. Tacking allowed us to make progress in our desired direction because we were sailing upwind and against the current, so it took us a couple of days to get there.

Life in Polynesia

A large triangle of islands stretches from Hawaii, to Easter Island, to New Zealand, and includes the French Polynesia island and other islands such as Samoa, Tonga, and Tuvalu and the Cook Islands. What I love about these islands are their very warm and loving society. No one is left out of activities or get-togethers, whether you are related by blood or not. People take care of other people's kids and each other. In fact, it is considered rude not to be included in any event or activity.

I wouldn't call it socialistic, but the survival, comfort, and care of the group is more important than the individual. Individuals do not want to stand out against others. Of course, you can have an opinion and say your piece, but when it comes to making decisions, it takes a long time to reach one because they want everyone to agree.

It is not like strict majorities or totalitarian systems, where all the rules and laws come from the top down. Rather, it is a society where the order of the groups and families have their input and say in what goes on. However, it takes time to process all of that and get different perspectives, for example, whether to chop down a tree, build a canoe, or sell things.

Once the decision is made, then pretty much everyone is in agreement, and most people are comfortable with the final decision, but it does take a while. It is really tough for people from Western cultures to go to Polynesia to get anything done because it is frustratingly long. They realize that there is always time to do things, no matter what, but they value family and social time more and make a point to listen to everyone's conversation and opinion.

In Hawaii, we ran into people all the time and always took a moment to stop and talk to them. No one is in a hurry, and they enjoy the interaction because they believe that is most important. In other words, relationships are more important than getting a house built.

When my sister was trying to build her house over there, if the surf was up, the workers were gone. No one would show up to work, so you have to account for surfing time. It certainly is not a very efficient way to get a house built, but everything is much more relaxed on the islands.

About 500 miles from the Line Islands is Penrhyn Island, also called Te Pitaka, Hararanga, Mangarongaro, or Tongareva, which is a northern group of the Cook Islands in the South Pacific. Penrhyn is a circular island that encloses a lagoon where we pulled in to anchor our sailboat. As we were anchoring, we could see all these yellow sharks swimming around us, and we immediately thought, "How are we going to get to the island?"

About a half hour later, a group of kids came out into the water to greet us, yelling and screaming, "Hello!"

Immediately, we asked one of the older ones about the yellow sharks, and he said, "Oh, don't worry about them. They are like puppy dogs. The ones you need to watch out for are the black sharks—they are not as friendly. The yellow sharks won't bite you."

They were so excited to see us because new people and things are rather scarce out there on the islands. This is where I would trade T-shirts from the States for natural pearls that they would find in the local oysters or in their cooking pots. They know they are valuable, but value to them is what is useful to them living on the island.

> *"I would trade T-shirts from the States for natural pearls."*

I recall the first time I went to Fanning Island, which was divided in two groups of 500 people; the majority of the people were Catholics, and the other half were Protestants. Even though I grew up Presbyterian, the Catholics always invited everyone to go to church. Since they didn't have a piano or organ, they all sang a cappella, which was wonderful to hear. The singing and harmonies were beautiful whether you were religious or not. I was the only one who went to the Protestant church with Pastor Joe, while the others went to the Catholic church.

The Bible was written in Kiribati language, which opens up the Word of God for people in their own language on the islands. The translation project started in 1988 with the translation of the

New Testament. Even though it took a while for the older generation to adjust to this new version, it helps the people better understand the message of the Gospel so they can study the living Word of God there.

New Zealand

Everywhere I travel, I always have interesting interactions with people. I always enjoyed going to New Zealand, which is a strong partner and friend of the United States. In fact, the US and New Zealand share common elements of culture, history, and a commitment to democratic principles, including the 1951 Australia-New Zealand-US (ANZUS) treaty, under which participants agreed to consult in case there was ever an attack in the Pacific and to meet that danger head-on.

However, this changed in the 1980s, when New Zealand implemented a policy barring nuclear-armed warships from its ports, preventing an alliance cooperation under ANZUS. In 1986, the US suspended its ANZUS security obligations to New Zealand but a decade later, in 2010, signed the Wellington Declaration, which provided guidance for security cooperation.

New Zealand actively engages in peacekeeping and international security efforts around the world. In fact, the US and New Zealand, including Christchurch, which is the staging area for joint logistical support, work together on a range of scientific areas. The US exports aircraft, machinery, vehicles, and optic and medical instruments. New Zealand imports meat, lamb, beverages such as wine and dairy products, machinery, and casein. Since 1992, the US and New Zealand have had a bilateral Trade and Investment Framework Agreement in place.

Over the years, I have noticed that there are more Hawaiians in California than in Hawaii, and there is a large group in Oregon and San Francisco. Why? There are more opportunities for them once they get exposed to Western culture and see the advantages of it. They get pulled into a consumer society, whereas in Hawaii they could live nicely off the land.

Fanning

When we first went to Fanning, they were only getting a supply ship once a year. Once they had more shipments coming in on a regular basis, they were more comfortable with that because before, they got rice, sugar, flour, coffee, tea, etc., only one time a year. Churches would buy a lot of supplies and distribute them to their members. We would always take extra staples that we would present to the churches. It was a great way to do that because you don't want to get too involved in giving products to just one person. It can create a conflict by aligning yourself with one family and can generate squabbles, so it is much better to give to the churches and let them distribute everything to the people as a thank-you for their hospitality.

In Fanning, we would anchor in the lagoon, have access to their water supply, and be able to fill our tanks on board. They would invite us to a feast and share what they had with us, so we shared things with them. That was the custom.

Fiji

In Fiji, when you leave the main island and head out to the outer islands, you have to go the chief first and ask permission to anchor off his island. There is a ceremony where you bring awa, a root that is crushed with water and makes a soupy, light brown mixture that has a slight numbing effect, often used in ceremonies. Plus, they take the awa root and pound it to create the drink kava, something they love to drink. When you go to an outer island, you have to ask permission to become a part of their village, and presenting awa to the chief is a great way to introduce yourself. He makes you a part of the village, and then you are free to go around the area, anchor, snorkel, and mingle with the village people.

These are customs that are important to observe because those who live there can get quite angry if you don't. In fact, they could easily ban you from the island and say, "No, we don't want you here." You don't want to cross them in any way, so you always come humbly with gifts of ava. If you show them respect for their island and customs, in turn, they will show you courtesy.

Solomon Islands

On another trip, I went to the Solomon Islands, which is actually a sovereign state that consists of six major islands and over 900 smaller islands that lie to east of Papua New Guinea and northwest of Vanuatu. Port Vila is the capital and the largest city of Vanuatu, where I flew in on the island of Espiritu Santo (which means "holy spirit"). From there, I took a dingy to another island near where the *Gershon II* was docked.

I met a friend of mine, Stephanie, who was a producer and ran a little program for Outer Voices, a non-profit organization which produces programs for public radio around the world like our National Public Radio (NPR) in the USA. She came with us to the Solomon Islands because she wanted to interview female navigators, something Steve and I have always been interested in. She hired us to take her to Taumako Island, which is more Polynesian than Melanesian. I came along to help with the trip, and she interviewed Steve and me for her show, *Blue Water Cowboys*, a quite popular NPR show. In the early days, the monarch of Hawaii adopted Taumako as part of Hawaii and the Polynesian family of islands.

Local transportation Taumako Island, Solomons

One of the most interesting ladies I have ever met is Mimi George, wife of David Lewis, who wrote a book called *We, the Navigators*. Born in Plymouth, England, he was a sailor, adventurer, doctor, and Polynesian scholar. He was raised in New Zealand and Rarotonga and developed an appreciation for Polynesian culture. He is best known for his studies of the traditional systems of navigation used by the Pacific Islanders. His published studies in *We, the Navigators* inspire a revival of traditional voyaging methods in the South Pacific.

In 1960, he soloed on his first trans-Atlantic yacht race from Plymouth to the East Coast on a 25-foot steel boat named *Ice Bird*. Later, he sailed around the world with his wife and two daughters on that boat to Antarctica, spending a year on the ice. In addition, his long-lasting interest in old navigational methods was used to explore the Pacific without the use of a compass, sextant, or marine chronometer.

Steve, Cheryl, and me on Gershon II *at Taumako Island, Solomons*

Along with Dr. Marianne (Mimi) George, he suggested that original Polynesian navigation is still alive in the Polynesian outliers, a number of culturally Polynesian societies that geographically lie outside the main region of Polynesian influence. Polynesian outliers are scattered in the two other Pacific subregions, Melanesia and Micronesia, which are considered to have been colonized by seafaring Polynesians.

I had met Mimi though Nancy, so our paths kept crossing over the years as she was working with the people on Taumako Island. She had sailed down there on her own boat, sold it, and built a double-hulled canoe with the islanders to develop a transport system so they wouldn't have to depend on the tugboats from the capital. The village built the boat, and she was supportive of that and encouraged it. To build a boat on an island like that, the very first thing you have to do is grow a garden, in order to feed the people who are building the boat. Most people don't think of doing something like that, but you have to feed the people who are going to do the work.

Mimi, Gregory, and me on Gershon II

Our mission was to take Stephanie to interview a female navigator, then pick up Mimi so she could get back home. We joined the boat and sailed to Lata, Ndeni, the capital of the outer eastern islands, Santa Cruz Islands, then to Solomon Islands, before meeting on Taumako Island. We had to anchor outside the reef after sailing all night and then decided to go ashore. Some of us hopped on board with Mimi and surfed through the channels and waves before continuing on to the village.

When we got to the village, all 70 people on the island showed up to welcome us. They sang to us and gave us food, and, though I was exhausted, I was overwhelmed with emotion. Soon after, they took us to a guest house and said, "You have had a long sail—you rest," and brought us food that included fish, yams, and rice.

One of the natives came to me and said, "You're Western" and handed me a pillow.

Of course, I said thank you and was grateful for the hospitality, but I always travel with a lava-lava cloth pillow, just in case. A lot of men wear it around their body or use it to cover them up at night.

Soon, I ate some food and went right to sleep for two hours. When I woke up, I immediately started looking for fresh water and found it pouring down from a mountain stream, bathed, and rinsed off. As far as going to the bathroom, I had to go down to the beach, dig a hole, do my business, and then the ocean would wash it out.

The Chief Kavea who lived there was 90 years old. He lived there with his wife, Cecilia, and they offered us big bowls filled with rice and fish. The rule is you eat some of it, then pass it on to the next person. It was actually quite tasty and delicious. We talked a bit and then had a little dance where everyone joined in and moved to the rhythm of the music. There were some guys beating on a hollowed-out log, so we could do rhythm dancing in the glow of the fire. It was amazing. If you are willing to relax, be adaptable, and accept the fact that there are people out there who mean you no harm, then you can have lovely experiences with some amazing people.

> *"Stephanie interviewed a 103-year-old navigator."*

Eventually, we left there with the chief and Cecelia and sailed to another little island, Nifiloli. We anchored off a reef there to get people ashore, and there Stephanie interviewed a 103-year-old navigator. Her interview served as documentation on how women are a big part of the active life of sailing and navigation. Even though women have been actively participating in sailing, they never received any recognition for their work. My friend wanted to document her life experiences as a woman navigator to show that women have made important contributions to sailing.

We took the chief and Cecelia back to the island and then went on to another island where they have saltwater crocodiles. You definitely have to be careful swimming in that area, and when we asked whether there were any crocs around, they said no.

However, after we swam for a while, we saw a guy who said, "I just saw a croc." Saltwater crocs will swim from island to island, and this was happening on Solomon Island, which was a different world.

The World War II Battle of Guadalcanal was the first major victory for the US Marines, who launched a surprise attack in August of 1942 and took control of an air base that was under construction. Eventually, the Japanese suffered a greater toll of casualties and withdrew from Guadalcanal by February of 1943.

Possession of a Guadalcanal air base was very important to control the sea lines of communication between the US and Australia. The ship losses were heavy on both sides, but Japan lost an elite group of naval aviators and could no longer withstand the counteroffensive of the powerful US military.

My Solomon Island trip happened in 2006, and my mom had moved to Hawaii in 2000. By this time, she was in her 90s and had memory issues. I met with her doctor, who gave specific instructions so I could take her back to California to visit with her grandsons and nieces. We were up in Sausalito and went out to lunch on a Friday. On Saturday, the next day, she started to feel ill and passed away a couple of days later. Fortunately, she had been easy to take care of and loved to travel and have people over, so she never felt uncomfortable or isolated. She led a good life.

Chapter 6

HELPING YOUNG PEOPLE CONNECT TO THE SEA

Although this may be off the subject of sailing, George Orwell warned us about the government, or the controlling powers at be, where computers, phones, and televisions would be in front of everyone's face, leading to what we would relate to, instead of each other. It was his projection of the future, and it is definitely coming true.

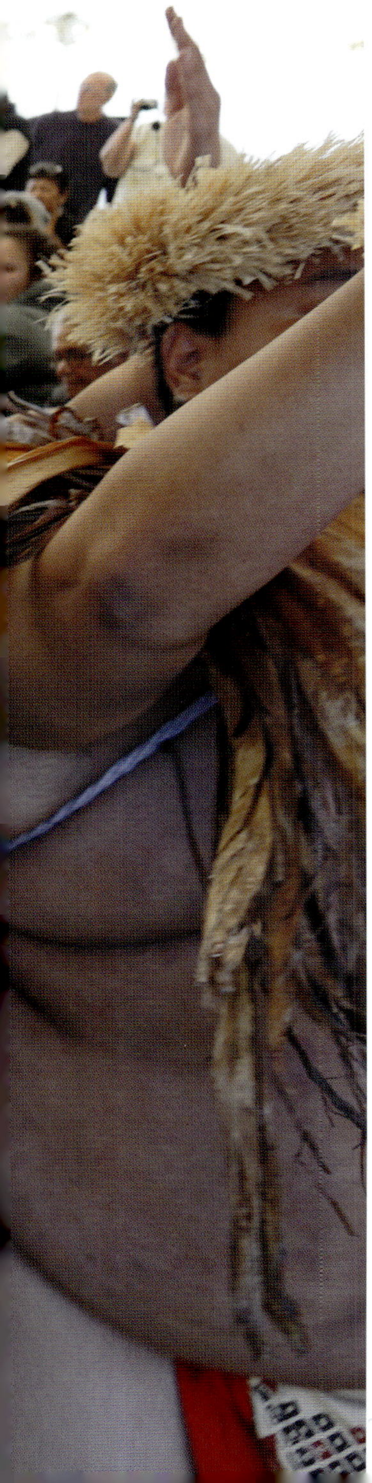

Maori Ceremony with the children for the departure of Hokulea *from New Zealand*

His novel *1984* shouts out in protest against totalitarianism and a loss of language and collective memory or history. He always warned about the danger of letting too much power flow into the hands of too few people because it can lead to abuse and force people to do what they hate to do. This can also be seen today with everyone on their cell phone, people sitting down to dinner with family at a restaurant and pulling out their phone instead of talking to each other.

From the culmination of where I came from, sailing all over the world and getting involved with helping young people get connected to the sea, this is my way of combating this phenomenon. Getting involved with Call of the Sea, founded in 1985 by Alan Olson and a group of local sailors, is an opportunity for kids in the Bay Area to sail traditionally rigged vessels while learning about maritime history and marine environment, inspiring them to become stewards of the earth and sea.

Call of the Sea's mission is to provide access to science-based educational programs that foster the connection to nautical heritage, the ocean, and watersheds. The organization wants to empower students of all ages and backgrounds to become stewards of the environment and transform their world throughout on-the-water field experiences.

In 2004, a new group of committed sailors came together to purchase the schooner *Seaward*, which has now served over 50,000 students (an average of 5,000 students per year) ever since through sailing trips each year. In January of 2015, the Educational Tall Ship, Inc. (ETS) was constructed called the *Matthew Turner* in Sausalito, California. The 132-foot wooden ship also serves as a floating classroom for students, serving the Northern California community and beyond.

Throughout all the projects, the kids have to put away their cell phones, which teaches them how to communicate with each other, work together as a team cohesively, and get familiar with the ocean environment, including all the critters, birds, and fish.

We have over 200,000 hours of volunteer labor, which is worth about $5–$6 million in manual labor alone. Plus, the lumber for the ship was brought to us through conservation groups who manage timberlands. At one point, we had a board maker who would make the boards right on site in Sausalito. We had all these talented people, including our captain, Adrian, who is an experienced rigger and worked to rig the *Matthew Turner* based on a 1891 ship called the *Galilee*. It had one of the fastest passages from Tahiti to San Francisco.

> "...there is a whole world out there that functions without media."

After eight long years, we were finally getting the boat out on the San Francisco Bay. We are planning to get our certification by the Coast Guard by April 2020, and that would license us to take up to 80 people out per sail, or 30 kids a night for overnighters with 38 bunks on board. It would be considered a school trip for Call of the Sea, with the intention of using the ship for all of our school programs.

When the *Matthew Turner* was launched over a weekend, I went up on Friday and stayed until Monday, but I made a point of staying away from the media. Mind you, I am not against television; in fact, I enjoy PBS and watching movies, but the news is so often redundant and creates hysteria, making everyone anxious. On my trips, I like to get up early, build a roaring fire, sit around the fireplace, read books, and make delicious food—and, for me, that is a vacation.

In all my years of sailing, to all sorts of different islands and remote places, I've realized there is a whole world out there that functions without media. They enjoy happy and successful lives with wonderful relationships in their community and family groups without being intruded upon with all the misery and disasters that are going on in the world. The focus is on each other, the community, the island, and how they function. You are much more useful and integral to the success of each other than you are in staying in that high state of anxiety over what is going on in the rest of the world. It is so wonderful to be out there and experience such a disconnect from the craziness of the world.

Part of our education programs involves yoga, which also puts students in a situation removed from their cell phone, computer, and technology. Let's face it: when you listen to CNN or some of the news channels constantly, it heightens your state of anxiety, keeping you in a disturbed state. Why do so many people let that happen? You have a choice—you do not need to know what is going on in the news all the time. It doesn't mean you have to be uninformed, but you can take a break from it all on a regular basis.

My favorite way to get the news is to read the paper, taking my time and reading what I want to read, such as interesting stories, editorials, or the local paper. Whatever is going on in Orange County has always interested me because my family has been involved in medical buildings in that area forever.

As I am writing this book, we are still in the middle of a quarantine for COVID-19. My business partner's husband happens to be a scientist from the University of Irvine (UCI). He texted me a picture of a chart that showed the comparison between the coronavirus and the flu, and he said, "Give these to your clients. The flu has been around forever with flu epidemics every year that affect the young and old due to their weakened immune systems Sometimes they lose their lives, but we don't see the world panicking over that and everyone to be quarantined."

That made me realize how much healthier, peaceful, and real it is being out sailing in the islands with the opportunity to deal with the local people. I grew up in Los Angeles, San Francisco, and Hawaii and certainly am not a stranger to urban life, but I really appreciate the difference between living out there on the islands versus the urban life living day to day. I am used to it and know how not to get trapped or let it bother me.

Following Hokulea *to Australia crossing, Tasman Sea*

For example, you never see homeless people in Polynesia because everyone is taken care of and is assimilated into village life, so it is a very inclusive society. Whereas in the US, we are all individualistic and don't think that way.

The last big expedition I did was in 2006 with a couple who were working on *Gershon II* and later in 2014, when they were working as crew escorting the Hawaiian *Hokulea* (*Hoku* means "star" and *lea* means "bright" and stands for the star Arcturas) on its around-the-world voyage that took three years. I went on the first escort from New Zealand to Australia, which was wonderful and took about two weeks.

In 2017, I flew to Tahiti to work with Steve on the last leg of the voyage from Tahiti back to Hawaii. The students or the navigators on the canoe determined the course and used traditional navigation to figure out where they were headed. In 2014, it was from Mangonui, an old whaling port on the eastern side of New Zealand near the upper northern tip facing the Tasman Sea.

Hokulea *crew from New Zealand to Australia, May 2015 (from left to right): Miguel, Terry, Bob, Cheryl, Steve, and Bill*

Before we departed from Mangonui, we had a beautiful ceremony with the people up there on compound at the northern part of New Zealand that overlooked the ocean. It had a large circle that pointed to the different star directions that they used as a teaching method for students. It was a huge event for the Hawaiians to have a ceremony for all participants connected with the sail and with the Maori, the local indigenous people of New Zealand.

The New Zealanders and the Maori created a treaty of Waitangi on the eastern northern coast that granted independence within the Maori to the government with their own land and lodge houses. Earlier on than most other places, the Maori had gained the respect of the white immigrants or Europeans who came to settle.

We departed Mangonui with *Hokulea* and sailed across the Tasman Sea heading toward Sydney, Australia, but we had gale-force winds, so we went into the harbor north of Sydney known as Coffs Harbor, and that is where we docked. It just so happened that I ran into an English lady, Suzi, who had her boat there and whom I hadn't seen in years. She knew our boat right away because sailors take care of sailors.

I managed to have her take my place because I was leaving with my friend Bill, allotting enough time for our trip. Steve knew I was leaving, and I asked Suzi to replace me on the trip to Brisbane. When we were sailing from New Zealand to Australia, Steve asked me about Bill's credentials and level of experience for that leg.

I looked him right in the eye and replied, "Well, he doesn't get seasick and eats anything."

It was a great experience, especially finding that old friend Suzi, getting her to replace me on the boat up to Brisbane, as they moved north into Queensland and up to Darwin before heading to Indonesia, the Indian Ocean. The sail was an incredible around-the-world journey, but I could only do those two sails, or two legs of the trip.

I helped out on the first and last leg from Tautira, the end tip of Tahiti, a very traditional Tahitian village where the chief came down to the boat to greet us at a place where we could get fresh water and wash and dry our clothes. His whole face was tattooed and looked very imposing, yet he was the nicest man you would ever want to meet, and I had a great time talking with him. Some of these Hawaiians are huge people in stature and look very intimidating, but they are very kind and have good hearts.

They recognized that we were volunteers in support of the revival of their culture, of sailing and navigational traditions of Polynesia. I love giving back to the community in Hawaii because everyone there was always so nice to me, and that is why I started working with the Polynesians and Tahitians, including those in Tahiti. I always tell people that French Polynesia is the center of my universe—it is the most wonderful place to be, in addition to enjoying the beauty of the islands due to the French influence. We enjoyed fresh baguettes and croissants every morning and excellent fish and rice, one of my favorite dishes. And I always feel comfortable there.

Australia
South Pacific
Stars Planets Galaxies
The Ocean Sailing Yacht

Suzi, Cheryl, and me in Coffs Harbor, Australia

Gershon II *crew in Coffs Harbor, Australia*

In New Caledonia, the largest island of the French overseas in the southwestern Pacific Ocean, about 750 miles east of Australia, there is a patisserie called George's that serve the most delicious Napoleons. Being so removed from Western society in the tropics and South Pacific, to be able to go into this wonderful pastry store and eat a Napoleon was truly amazing. It is like traveling and missing your favorite food from back home, unexpected, and such an indulgence especially after getting off the boat.

Steve had a fridge and freezer on board, but they were limited to frozen chicken and fish, so these little luxuries of fresh pastries were such a delight. Kona has great coffee because of the altitude, and Fiji has a large Indian population, so you can buy wonderful curry powders in the marketplace, and that was always a nice treat. Since the English couldn't get people to come and work their plantations, they brought Indians to do the work. That is why there is such a large Indian population in Fiji and access to curry and curry powders is in abundance there.

Those were my last big sails in 2007 and 2014. In 2019, I joined Steve in Canada at Vancouver Island for a week near Queen Charlotte Sound, but that was the last overnight sail. Nowadays, I don't have the time and don't want to leave my dog for that long. When I was younger, I had a fishing boat and a 90-pound Alaskan malamute who I would row ashore to walk and let her do her business, but I was a lot younger then and more energetic.

Lucky fisherman catching mahi-mahi from New Zealand to New Caledonia

For a variety of reasons it becomes an issue having a dog on board, especially crossing oceans. Feeding a dog can become a serious problem, as well as letting them go to the bathroom, where you run the risk of them falling overboard. A lot of times, dogs will disappear overnight, tumbling overboard, if the boat lurches suddenly or the animal gets in the wrong location on the boat. It is hard to explain to them where it is safe and where it is not safe. Plus, it is hard to watch them 24-7 when you are so busy doing other stuff, especially if there is a squall or bad weather. I never really wanted to do that. Plus, it is hard to exercise a dog on a sailboat. To be honest, a cat would be a better option for a pet on a sailboat.

Over the years, between here and Catalina, people have occasionally found a dog out in the water that you knew fell off a boat somewhere. Every so often, about every couple of years, I would hear a story about someone discovering a dog out in the water and had no idea where it came from. Thank goodness for the ones that are found. It is difficult unless you have a big boat where you could have a little dog room with a potty area. There have been people who cruise up and down the Delta in the San Francisco Bay area that tie up at night and go for walks with their dogs. While they make great companions on your boat, you definitely have to take precautions for safety when it comes to pets.

Safety is also important for all who are on board. One time, we were coming back up from Tahiti in calm waters with a little bit of wind and just sailing along. When the conditions are like that, it is a good time to take a bath by getting buckets of seawater to bring on board. Instead, this guy decided he was going to dip himself in the water off the edge of the boat, but he got swept away. There we were, sailing away, with this naked man in the water, so I immediately did a jibe ho and went back to get him in the wide-open ocean. It took about 15 minutes to do so, but we were able to keep tabs on his location and eventually picked him up out of the water. The moral of the story is you have to be careful out there.

I heard of another overboard situation with a friend of mine who was losing her vision but was determined to go on a four-month cruise around Africa. Since her sister had recently lost her husband, they both thought it would be a good time to go on a long cruise. Before arriving back in Fort Lauderdale, Florida, from one of the islands, her sister jumped overboard, committing suicide. The police and FBI were called in, and she had no idea her sister was so depressed. She was devastated but eventually posted some beautiful pictures from so many wonderful places they shared on their trip. She finds it so odd that on the last leg of their trip, her sister felt compelled to end her life. No one quite understands it.

Another situation happened that I didn't understand either when we were sailing the inner islands from Maui to Hawaii with an artist friend. We were right in the middle of the channel with deep seas when all of the sudden, she came out on deck, totally naked, and was almost blown overboard. One of the crew grabbed her and took her down below, and she seemed OK after that incident. When we arrived in port, she drew a panoramic picture of the volcanoes, but she sure gave us all quite a scare.

"We had a great time."

Chapter 7

MORE SAILING ADVENTURES

As I write this chapter, the COVID-19 pandemic is in full force throughout the world as we were coming back from a trip to Hawaii. My nephew had rented a house on the island, my one friend and her two kids rented another place right on the water, and my other two friends stayed with me. We had a great time making dinners together, having a catered pool party, boating, swimming, kayaking, snorkeling, and simply enjoying the island and being together. The markets were open, and we had plenty of food and drink. Since I had not been there in a while, I was grateful that I had stocked up on toilet paper and paper towels before the pandemic set in, items that have become rather scarce.

ROXY

My oldest nephew, his wife, and two boys, plus the two daughters of my youngest nephew, Tyler

With the government restrictions, everyone is required to have a two-week quarantine when entering the United States. As a result, many tourists did not want to travel, so many of the airplanes were flying empty, and all the hotels were closed. The tourist industry has been badly damaged as hotel and restaurant workers are struggling to make ends meet. And since there would be much fewer supplies coming into the states with shortages, including medical supplies, I thought it would be easier for me to be in Newport Beach rather than in the Pacific.

The senior population is most vulnerable to the virus, but when I got to Hawaii, there were no cases of the coronavirus, but by the time I left, there were five cases. I found out that the coronavirus had gone through Hawaii in December of 2019 already, so they were somewhat immune to catching it again. In fact, the big island is probably one of the safest places to be right now since the markets have plenty of food, including fresh fruits and vegetables.

Every year, the islands are at risk for hurricanes, so the people are used to going into survival mode. However, since the island is so high, it is often able to deflect these hurricanes, as they move south or north or avoid the island altogether. The last big hurricane to hit the Big Island of Hawaii was about 150 years ago which traveled between Maui and the Big Island but Kauai had been hit by hurricane "Eva" in 1982 and hurricane "Iniki" in 1992.

The lower islands are more vulnerable that are just under the Tropic of Cancer at 22.5 degrees north, with the Tropic of Capricorn at 22.5 degrees south, which determines the tropics. We are just at the edge, right next to the big island, and that is 19 degrees north, so Hawaii is considered subtropical. When you are in the tropics, that is where the hurricanes form; they usually come out of Baja California in southern Mexico and run north and west, or otherwise they will stream across the Pacific, threatening us from below, depending on El Niño conditions.

I have lived through so many hurricanes, so I, too, have that survival mentality, and we were definitely lucky to be able to get to Hawaii before the government restrictions got too strict. At home in Newport Beach, I am grateful that I can use DoorDash to get food, or anything else I need, delivered to my door.

Since my love for all these islands never ends, starting in 2013, I started focusing on educating my nephews on where I sailed. It all started with a group of us talking about going to Antarctica. My friend Steve and I always dreamed of doing a sailing trip there and really thought we would eventually do that trip, but it never happened.

Death Valley Eagle Mine, April 2014, for Santa Barbara City College

As a result, I found myself being able to go on the *Explorer* ship with a group of National Geographic scientists who were going to do research in Antarctica. While on board, they gave lectures about the environment, so it turned out to be somewhat of an educational trip, too. It was 2014 when I put that trip together with my friends Steve and Cheryl Kornberg, Jeff Miller, and another couple, Lauren and Steve Gertz.

We flew from Newport Beach to Bogota, Columbia, and spent the night there—it's about 7,000 feet high in altitude—before flying to Buenos Aires, and then Argentina, where we spent the day, and then continued on to Ushuaia in Argentina, the very tip of South America. From Beagle Channel, we embarked on the *Explorer* for a 10-day sail across the Drake Strait to the Antarctica Peninsula, and then we went below the Arctic Circle before coming back.

We had lovely weather and saw about six penguin colonies. It was rather surreal to be able to get off the boat and walk among them. Undisturbed by people, they didn't seem to mind us as strangers to their world. We saw killer whales, orcas, humpback whales, and all sorts of sea birds, and it turned out to be quite an educational trip.

As we traveled farther south, the ship actually beached itself, which allowed us to get off and walk on the ice. We walked right up to see Emperor penguins, the largest of their kind, as they are almost as tall as me, and we couldn't resist their comical and cute personalities. As far as the eye could see, we saw thousands and thousands of penguins. I was fulfilling a dream of visiting this awe-inspiring Antarctica but was also grateful for traveling in a quite comfortable manner.

We finally arrived at Port Lockroy, a British station that has a small post office where you can mail cards and letters. Though it is a very isolated area, there was a 60-foot ship that I had thought about sailing on to Antarctica. I actually knew people who had sailed there on their 50-foot boat in 1962; Nancy and Bob Griffith, with their son Reed, had circumnavigated Antarctica. That took 109 days and was the fastest circumnavigation ever, a record that landed them in the *Guinness Book of World Records*. The stories that she used to tell me about Antarctica made me want to go there all the more.

On board the *Explorer*, there was one dining room, one bistro, one store, and one gym, without a lot of other amenities. There was a big salon that was used for lectures—a very simple place but quite comfortable. I managed to get a large cabin that was on the back of the boat, and I had a little balcony overlooking the stern.

While we were there, Teno, Nancy's son, gave me some of her ashes, and we had a little ceremony for her off the balcony while pouring her ashes in the Antarctica waters. Since it was a favorite spot of hers, I thought it would be nice to do that for Nancy and her family, as she was such a special lady. Mind you, we had to do it secretly and couldn't let the captain know what we were up to. We managed to create a wonderful memorial as everyone gathered on the balcony and hummed a Hawaiian song in her memory. It was quite touching.

EXPLORER

Andvord Bay, Danco Isle, January 21, 2014, in Antarctica

Weddell Sea, Paulet Island, January 2014, in Antarctica

Visiting the penguins

My mentor's son, Teno, who is also a close friend (and I am godfather to his son, Gabe), had put together a film that his parents took of their early sailing days. The film is titled *Following Seas* and can be accessed on Vimeo online. Check it out because it documents some of their amazing sailing adventures. The film's cover photo is of when they got shipwrecked on an atoll in the Tuamotus and salvaged as much of their boat, the *Awahnee*, as possible. They packed it up over a period of six months while living off the island with two French Polynesian prisoners. They finally got back to Tahiti and then New Zealand, where they built a ferrocement boat similar to their old one and continued to sail two more circumnavigations after it was finished.

Terry, Teno, and Nancy

On my next trip to New Zealand, I invited both my nephews, but it turned out to be Eric and his family who joined me. We stayed on a 6,000-acre working ranch called Kauri Cliffs that overlooked the water on the north island, about an hour north of Russell. There were beaches and a golf course, and, combined with a cattle and sheep operation, it made for a lovely place. I wanted them to see Russell, a popular place for sailors, so we took a ferry boat over there, then took a side trip to Mangonui, north of the ranch. There at that old Australian whaling port we had the best fish and chips.

"I wanted to share special places with my family and friends who normally would not have thought about going to these sites and areas of the world."

I was comfortable not always sailing on a boat by going to these places in different ways just because they were so special to me. It didn't matter what mode of transportation we took; I just wanted to share these places with my family and friends who normally would have never thought about going to these sites and areas of the world.

Sharing my love of sailing with my nephew's children

The second time I went to New Zealand, I took my youngest nephew, his wife, and their two daughters, and my friends Jeff, Muffy, and Monica. With eight of us in our group, we flew to Napier, New Zealand, which is a little farther south on the north island, and we stayed for three days at another ranch on the water called Kidnappers.

From there, we flew to Queenstown, on the South Island, and stayed at a little lodge on a beautiful lake. Helicopters flew us up into the Southern Alps; we landed on a glacier before going over to the ocean side, where we landed on the beach. Before having lunch, we got to hit biodegradable golf balls into the water. It was an amazing trip. The golf course near the lake in Queenstown has a reputation for being a great golf course, and since my nephew loves to play golf, he was in heaven. Having heard so many good things about these places, I felt good about giving him the opportunity to play there.

While my nephew Tyler and his wife, Kelly, played golf, the rest of us, including their daughters Nicki and Gilliann, friends Elizabeth Hersey, Monica McQueen, and Jeff Miller, and I, went to an old gold mining place across town, and then we came back to the restaurant at Jack's Golf Course, where we enjoyed the best seafood we ever had. Big beautiful oysters from the southern end of the island were just shucked, and my friend Monica and I had two platters before being served the fish and chips. Who would have thought that a little-known golf course restaurant would have such great food?

We also went on the Dart River in a speed boat that roared around doing 360s. It is such an unspoiled, clean, sparsely populated area, unlike anywhere else you would see in the world. I love the Kiwi people because they are so understated and quite friendly.

The route we took from Napier allowed us to see a historic town filled with incredible Victorian buildings, something we loved since we had just found a 1928 home for my mom in Sausalito, California. It turned out to have a great view of the city and came with permits to build a garage, which we needed, so I asked the architect and builder to come and meet us to see what the original owner had planned out.

The architect, John Swain, turned out to be the commodore of the San Francisco Yacht Club, so he invited me to be in a schooner race, especially when he learned of my background and interest in sailing. While I was up there, I went on *Seaward*, an 82-foot steel boat owned by Call of the Sea, the nonprofit organization, that would be in the schooner races. Seaward also participated in the traditional Ancient Mariner races in San Francisco Bay.

> "It is wonderful to see young people amazed and excited about being out on the water."

When I went sailing, I met Alan Olson, who was telling me about a dream he had about building a large school ship. I shared his dream with my old partner in the hopes of forming a nonprofit in Hawaii, but it never became viable because we didn't have enough support and money from the community. It would have been problematic to do it, but it was still in the back of my mind. With all my years of sailing and experience, wouldn't it be nice to encourage other young people to get connected to this type of life?

It is important for them to experience it, because with navigation, you use mathematics, learn observations, engage in star gazing and celestial navigation, and learn about the weather, environment, and winds—the forces that move around the planet. They learn how that is all connected to the planet spinning, why the axis turns, how magnetic forces are connected to the solar system and its cosmic power.

That seemed to be a natural progression for me, with what I could do to help other young people hopefully have that type of experience. This was very meaningful to me and a way for me to express my gratitude for a life at sea. It is wonderful to see young people amazed and excited about being out there on the water, understanding the forces of how boats can go out in what looks like a dangerous environment and be perfectly comfortable, knowing it is survivable, and come back safely.

Through that connection in 2008 when I met Alan, I donated some money to the project that he had told me about, and it

> "It is important for them to experience it ... and the forces ... connected to the planet spinning ..."

> "... and its cosmic power."

snowballed until I became the major benefactor of Call of the Sea. It was and is the most beautiful community effort I have ever seen. We ended up with volunteers from all walks of life who put in over 200,000 hours of volunteer labor. The donations we received were from conservation groups from different lands that donated thousands of Douglas firs and oak lumbar used to build the ship.

We had support from the city and the Army Corps of Engineers, who allowed us to keep it at the dock. A local businessman had some spare land that he donated for us to build the ship. We used that land in Sausalito as an old shipyard. The incredible support from the city for permits, hundreds of volunteers, very talented people, and conservation groups made it all possible to build this ship.

We launched the 135-foot ship in the water on April of 2017 and took her over to the dock to finish putting the mast on, rigging, completing the interior, and doing all the compliance that we needed to do for the Coast Guard. The first sail that I got to go on was January 15, 2020, which was very exciting. We went on another sail on February 29, 2020, a leap year, and had the most amazing sail with strong winds, all the sails up, heeling over, as we flew by the Golden Gate Bridge.

Basically, that is what we will be doing with her by offering schools, classes, and eventually some overnighters and some long-range trips. We have wonderful relationships at Dana Point, Newport Beach, and Catalina Islands Conservancy; all are very interested in doing some projects with us at the sea base in Newport Beach that is run by the Boy Scouts. Those are things that we are hoping to do once this COVID-19 pandemic is over.

Last night I watched two documentaries: one on the flu epidemic in 1918 that killed a lot of people and the second one that took place in the 1940s and '50s with the polio epidemic. There was an effort to turn the tide of that infection, but there were a lot of people who got polio that yielded some long-lasting effects. It was frightening and scared a lot of people.

March of Dimes was formed to raise a million dollars in dimes to help fight polio by finding a vaccine. President Franklin D. Roosevelt's personal struggle with polio led to the creation of the National Foundation for Infantile Paralysis, better known as the March of Dimes. They pioneered the vaccine research leading to the elimination of polio in the US and then shifted their focus to address other health threats to moms and babies, with innovations like folic acid, newborn screening, and surfactant therapy to treat respiratory distress syndrome.

Since I had caught polio when I was three, before there was any vaccine, I feel lucky that I survived it. I was quarantined, and it was very painful because my muscles ached, especially when I had to exercise or be bathed. These pandemics mark different parts of our past that we have all had to endure, and that is what we are going through now. It is the mark of the times.

"... go with the flow."

Chapter 8

STILL LOVE THE SEA

Meditation is becoming more popular these days, and my most effective way to do that is with a walking meditation that involves movement because it is easier for my mind to become still. It is very effective for handling the movement on a sailboat, or any boat, for that matter. When sailing, it is always important to go with the flow, as your body becomes familiar with the movement of the sailboat. In other words, I become part of the boat, the winds, and everything around me. I found a level of peacefulness that you might find with meditation as I became one with the boat. You become a part of the whole action of sailing as opposed to fighting it.

Whenever I had people on my sailboat who became seasick, I realized that they were struggling against the motion, which makes them nauseous and sick. Instead of letting go and becoming part of that motion, they would strive and strain instead of going with the flow; that is what quiets everything down. Surfers also understand that connection with the movement of the waves, and that is why they love doing it. They get into that zone of harmony with their environment, even though it seems frightening to a lot of people, but it is all in the mind. It is not frightening if you accept and understand that power of the water and the waves.

Sailors love being out there on the water no matter what the conditions, and I always loved being on the water. After suffering from allergies and asthma as a kid, I found relief when I would get out on the ocean because of the fresh, clean air. I embraced that because I felt so much better and completely comfortable out there. I always look forward to that and was willing to get out there any time of day or night.

I wasn't using my sailboat because it became too complicated to find crew to work it. Trying to do everything myself was not something I wanted to do, and I no longer found it as relaxing. Finding people who were competent and experienced was becoming rarer, and I simply didn't enjoy taking the sailboat out by myself.

It is so wonderful to be on a sailboat with a crew who love to be out on the open water and know what they are doing. You can turn the wheel over to them or ask them to take a sail down without going through all the motions of trying to teach them something new. Sometimes they simply don't understand what you are talking about or can't figure out what you want them to do when it comes to working the equipment or hoisting the sails.

Alekona crew, Tahiti to Kona, 2002

A lot of sailors you find in various seaports tend to be coastal sailors instead of blue water sailors. There is a big difference between those who do offshore sailing and those who cross oceans. In Newport Beach, where I live, you find many experienced ocean sailors, but some of them just want to race for speed.

Since I am not into racing, I decided to donate my sailboat, *Alekona*, to the Call of the Sea organization (callofthesea.org).

The Alekona at Avalon Harbor Catalina Island, California

When you donate your boat to a nonprofit, they have to lease it out for three years before you can get your deduction on the vessel. My main purpose was to get the boat utilized since I wasn't using it. When I donated it, they found a couple who wanted to take the boat up to the arctic with some scientists to do some photography. Since my boat is made of steel and was built in New Zealand, it is the perfect sailboat to do this type of work. It is something that she was meant to do, and that made my happy.

Today, I have a little Boston whaler and will run around the bay or go out in the ocean. Here I am, 60 years later, doing the same thing I did as a young boy. I have friends here in Newport Beach and also in San Francisco where I can go sailing or serve as crew. I can steer and do sail work, but I don't have to be captain, so it is much more relaxing and enjoyable for me. Then I can get off the sailboat, thank them for the ride, and head home without the added responsibility of maintaining a sailboat. That is where I have graduated to: a place where I still love being on the water but have no responsibility for getting out there.

In July of last summer, I flew up to Vancouver Island and spent a week on my friends' Steve and Cheryl's boat, exploring the inside of Queen Charlotte Sound, a beautiful area with whales, eagles, seals, and bears. It was delightful. Nowadays, I do have a complication with my service dog, Akamai, whom I have had for 11 years now. Akamai means "clever and smart" in Hawaiian. Fortunately, I have a professional hula dancer friend of mine who comes and takes care of him. When I did my last trip from Hawaii to Tahiti in 2017, I was grateful she looked after him, because I was gone for 24 days.

She loves feeding Akamai, a black and tan Japanese Shiba husky. This type of dog is smart, calm, and clean, travels well, and is extremely devoted to an owner. Loyal to a fault, Akamai is very affectionate and easy to take care of.

Akamai (my faithful dog) and me in front of the ship Matthew Turner *that we built in Sausalito, beginning in 2008 with my meeting with Alan Olson, director of the nonprofit sailing school Call of the Sea*

Getting back to the whole process of sailing, it is something that merges your whole mind, body, and soul. If you really love it, you become absolutely religious about it, totally immersed in the sailing terms, weather conditions, and history. I have always seen the spiritual side of it because it connects you to the universe and brings you to a state of absolute harmony.

There have been other ways of achieving that state of pure bliss. When I was 14 years old, I remember marlin fishing on a boat, *Dorsal II*, on the Sea of Cortez in Baha. We were tagging and releasing fish so that scientists could trace where the fish had been if and when they got caught. All the marlin that were caught were tagged and released, except for one that we traded for a horseback ride into the mountains.

Years ago, when I went down there with my dad, we were on a 60-foot boat. I will never forget the whiff of Spanish omelets being prepared by the cook in the galley. In fact, the aroma wafted into the room where I was sleeping and woke me up in the morning. Immediately, I woke up and had an epiphany: this is what I wanted to do for the rest of my life. I love the sailing world, being out there on the water in the calmness, the serenity, and that state of being that comes with it. No doubt, mountain climbers, yogis, and even talented dancers find that in their movements: that point of connection that puts them in an elevated state. Well, I found that bliss being on the ocean.

Mahi-mahi fishing

Ever since then, my whole focus became to find a way to live my life as close to the ocean as possible. Besides backpacking and going out into the desert, the ultimate for me has always been being on a boat in the ocean. Traveling has always been comfortable for me, and I have enjoyed going out into the unknown. Some people don't like that, but I loved it and was fascinated by the process. Curious by nature, I have had an inquisitive mind my whole life, and I am never bored. I could sit here and be thinking about something, wondering about the weather, the birds, or whatever is around me.

No matter where I am, I find something fascinating to me; even the bad times, the processes of going through terrifying situations, I still find it very interesting to see what happens, how it transpires, and how to solve it. The same is true when I am on a boat, because I learned how the boat reacts in all sorts of weather conditions. For example, when you are familiar with a boat under a lot of different circumstances, you are able to handle it and bring yourself safely through any challenging situation.

Building the 135-foot sailboat the *Brigantine* in Sausalito was certainly a challenge and my biggest motivation for donating funds to help make that happen. The whole process of bringing hundreds of volunteers and a whole community together to build the ship was truly awe-inspiring. We had square sails installed on the ship instead of tapered sails, which would allow us to get more movement and speed while sailing the ship.

For example, when you are slightly off the wind, you can get a lot more power than with a Marconi rig or a fore and aft sail. It takes more work and involvement, but the reason we did that is because it is a school ship and creates a lot of interesting and dynamic action, and it makes it possible to handle a more complicated rig with more bodies. The main purpose for building it was to teach and expose children, and anyone really, to something that I found so rewarding in my life—sailing. Since that is what I know, that is what I did.

Of course, other people may do other things that are just as valid, but for me, I learned about life by being on the ocean. The ocean is always moving, the air is never quite still, the universe is never stagnant, and all of that is cosmic power and motion. If you can work in harmony with that, there is something sublime about it all. Helping to get the *Brigantine* ship built was my way of sharing my passion for sailing with others.

The Alkenoa *in Avalon at Catalina Island*

It is important for an older person to help others by giving to young people something of value, something that they have learned in their lives. Isn't that the highest purpose—for someone older to teach a young person something that they can embrace and improve their lives for the better? It has been so rewarding for me to have my sailboat, *Alekona*, that I bought in New Zealand and spent so much time on—my last sailboat—now available for young people who want to experience the arctic. How wonderful.

Anyone who has owned a sailboat wants to see what their boat can do, and I feel lucky that it fell in the hands of people who understand its value and how strong and capable it is while handling challenging weather conditions that can help them do the work they want to do. I am proud to say that 70,000 miles were sailed on the *Goodewind*, from January 1984 to 2002.

Eventually, the *Goodewind* sailboat was too old to carry liability insurance or hull insurance, so I had to get rid of it. I remember finding her online as I looked at pictures of boats for sale and was willing to go anywhere to get the right sailboat. I found only three steel boats: one was in Spain, one was in Australia, and the *Alekona* was in Wellington, Australia.

The sailing vessel Goodewind *that we used for 20 years of sailing in Oceania, mostly in the Line Islands and French Polynesia and, of course, interisland about 100 times in Hawaii*

I had a sail from Fiji to Tauranga, New Zealand with Steve and Cheryl. When I saw a picture of it, I flew down to Wellington and put an offer in that was accepted. I sailed her back from Wellington to Tauranga, where I equipped her for an ocean passage, which included radar, an autopilot system, and a weather radio with single side bands, and I had a dodger made around the companion way.

At the time, the exchange rate was 2.5 to 1, so that made it more reasonable to purchase. Then I put a crew together and sailed for Tahiti. We had beautiful passages and were very lucky with the weather, and though we allowed three weeks for the sail, we made it in a little over two weeks. We allowed another three weeks from the passage to the big island, but we also made it in two weeks. I spent a week in Tahiti to replace the crew and provisioning.

"Captain Alverson ran a captain's school."

Chapter 9

HOW TO GET A CAPTAIN'S LICENSE

My teacher, Captain Alverson, a friend of Nancy's, ran a captains' school in order to train captains for all sorts of boats and ships. Over the years, he had trained over 80% of fishing charter captains, sailing captains, and tour boat captains in the state, with his base of operation in Honolulu. He would also go to the outer islands to teach the classes to those who wanted to become a captain.

Now that we had our sailboat and were going to run it as a business, Nancy encouraged me by saying, "You have to get your captain's license." Even though it wasn't on my radar at the time, I did have all the sea time required that I had accomplished since my early youth.

When I applied for my license, captains were required to have two years of sea time working as crew on a boat, and each day had to be a 24-hour day, which translated into 720, 24-hour days of sea time. I had to have that to qualify, and then I was taught all sorts of things that a captain would need to know. By then, I already knew how to navigate. In fact, when I met Nancy, she was teaching a celestial navigation course. I have always been fascinated with navigation and knew how to navigate with a sextant.

When you take a captain's course, you have to learn the rules of the road. For example, when navigating at night, the lights on other boats are the first clue as to what is in front of you. And your navigation lights are the first line of safety in order to avoid any collisions in the dark. In other words, your lights notify other vessels what you are and what you are doing.

If you are motoring a small vessel, red and green (port and starboard) lights are required as well as a white light that is visible around your boat in all directions. This is a stern light and a masthead light on sailboats. Any boat under sail requires a port light and a starboard light, with one stern white light. Any sailboat below 65 feet must show a tricolor light at the masthead instead of on the side and stern when sailing. When you are motoring, you have to have the lower lights.

When you are sailing out of a marina, for example, the green light in the bay will be on your right, or starboard, side. A red light will be on your port side. A good rule of thumb to remember is "Red-Right-Returning," except in French Polynesia, where it is the opposite, "Red-Right-on the Rocks."

Captain Alverson, founder of the Pacific Maritime Academy at the Coast Guard Base

If you decide to get your captain's license, you will also be taught different light configurations at night and what they mean. For example, when you have commercial ships, such as fishing boats, they will have certain lights on them to delineate what they are and what they are doing. You will be able to tell whether it is a fishing boat, tugboat, or barge. A tugboat will have lights that show the tug, and you will know that it is pulling a cable 600 feet behind it—something you do NOT want to cross when sailing. You must wait until the tug goes by.

In Hawaii, most of their goods and services are transported by tug and barges, so you have to be aware and stay alert for them because they have the right of way. There are larger container ships, but they go into Honolulu, and then the goods are reduced to smaller configurations on the barges that go to all the other harbors on the other islands.

The right of way is determined by the vessel with the most difficulty to maneuver, but it is not always necessarily that you have the right of way because you are on the starboard side. Typically, in pleasure boats, with boats of equal size such as power boats, sail boats usually have the right of way to a certain degree because they are following the wind. Power boats have better maneuverability, so whichever vessel has the best capability of maneuvering gives the right of way.

> ***"There was a 28-foot boat known as Curlew that sailed all the way around the world without an engine."***

Even if you are a small vessel and are coming near a bigger vessel, that does not mean you have the right of way. You can't expect to have the right of way with a cruise ship or tanker because it is difficult for them to maneuver. Therefore, you have to give way to the vessel that has the least maneuverability.

There are a lot of people out on the water who have not taken the captain's course (and should), but they think they do have the right of way, and that is not always true. Getting your captain's license involves taking a month-long course that will give you the rules of the road and teach you about navigation and how to recognize lights at night. You also have to take a first-aid course that must be renewed every year, including CPR. Once you receive it, the captain's license is good for five years. I have renewed it myself four times over 25 years.

Eventually, I took a radar course in Honolulu, which qualified me to use radar on a sailboat. As a captain, you can get qualified for power boats and sailboats, as well as how to operate radar, something that is extremely helpful at night with poor visibility, fog, and darkness. It is very useful when the wind is blowing onto the shore.

When you are in a sailboat, you are at risk and have to pay attention and be extra careful to keep your distance, often tacking away or doing some kind of maneuver. You can turn on your engine and use the sails at the same time to power your boat in the right direction. In the old days, engines were not an option, and it takes real talent and skill to maneuver a sailboat close to shore.

There was a 28-foot boat known as *Curlew* that sailed all the way around the world without an engine. I ran into a couple boats like that, and there were some French people I met who had sailed to Hawaii and Manele, a little tiny harbor on Lanai Island, where you have to time it just right when leaving the harbor. In fact, they had to use ropes to pull themselves out of the harbor. We sat in the harbor for two days, and all we could see was their mast bobbing up and down in the water because they couldn't go anywhere. That can be a problem when you don't have an engine, because you are totally dependent on the wind or water currents.

There was an interesting sailor from New England, named Irving Johnson, who dreamed of going to sea and would climb telephone poles pretending he was on top of the mast in a storm. It was 1929 when he got a position on board the *Peking*, a 400-foot barkantine barge out of Hamburg, Germany, that would travel through the North Sea down around South America. It was loaded with gravel that people in Chile would use for cement, and it would be replaced with grain before sailing back to Hamburg, all without an engine.

He took a box camera with him that he would hand crank to film his journey. In fact, there is a fascinating video showing how he climbed 17 stories to the top of the mast with his camera and filmed them going around the Cape Horn with the waves breaking and washing the decks. It is an exciting video, and he subsequently did quite a bit of sailing with his wife.

When I got my captain's license back in 1984, it cost $150, and the license would be granted after you presented all your credentials to the Coast Guard. My first license was for 100 tons, with sail endorsement determined by my experience. For a 100 gross ton license, 90 days must be on vessels of 51 gross tons or above, or 180 days must be on vessels of 34 gross tons or above. You have to take the extra test to qualify for sail endorsements, then you are tested before applying to the Coast Guard for your license. Captain schools will facilitate the process for you.

When you document sail time, it can be a little problematic because a lot of my sail time, I had to certify personally since I had done all this sailing time on all sorts of boats. Also, since I had my own boat, then you are considered the owner of a vessel, which qualifies you to be captain unless you have a licensed captain on board. The captain is responsible for anything that happens on board, whether there is damage to the sailboat or a collision, whether someone falls overboard, gets sick, or hurt, or anything like that, the captain is always responsible. If there is no captain on board, then the owner of the vessel is the responsible person.

When you become a captain, you are taking on a lot of duty and responsibility. That is why captains are notorious for being dictatorial, bossy, and blustery on board because they are the ones in charge and want everything done their way. As crew, you have to accept that.

When we worked for the University of Hawaii, Nancy, Steve, and I all had a captain's license, but we took turns being captain. When you think about it, there were three captains on board, but only one was in charge at a time, and everyone on board had to accept that fact. As much as we might rumble under our breath about a command or have gentle arguments, nevertheless, we understood that only one person could be captain. Whatever that captain wanted to do, that is what we had to do. But we were all reasonable people and focused on safety and the quality of the experience for everyone. You can't just let that captain power go to your head.

With that said, there is an upside to having three captains on board because you have a lot of experienced opinions about course, direction, which sail to put up, and so on. It is not like you can't consult with each other, and it gives you some options about what to do. As captain, I used to sail with a very experienced crew and hardly had to tell them anything. All I had to say was, "Let's leave, toss the lines, and get ready to go," or "It's time to put up some sail," or "Let's put up the main first."

The order of tasks might be different, but you might still ask someone, "Should we put up a bigger jib or a smaller one?" A discussion may ensue, but one person, the captain, has to make the decision. If there is only one captain, you can still have a discussion, but the captain is responsible for the safety of the vessel, everyone on board, and the job they are doing.

It doesn't matter where in the country or the world you get your captain's license—start documenting your sea time. In different countries, there might be different requirements for qualifying to get your captain's license. For example, there are maritime schools in Germany, England, and France where you can attend and graduate from if you want to make a career as a captain, whether it is for the navy, military, or commercially. In the outer islands of Hawaii, there was a man who would offer classes at a hotel for those who wanted to get their captain's licenses in that area of the world.

Getting a captain's license opens up opportunities for all sorts of jobs and experiences on both federal and nonfederal waters. It takes at least eight weeks to get your license if you are working with a captain's school. If you are operating a private boat, most insurance companies will not let you operate it without a captain's license, as they want someone with needed experience to minimize risk.

You have to have at least 360 days of boating experience, and 90 days must be in the past three years. You have to be at least 18 years old, complete a first aid and CPR certification, and have a physical completed within the last 12 months of applying for your captain's license.

Being a licensed captain is a great source of pride and pleasure for me. I have enjoyed working with all sorts of people around the world, including students, scientists, and teachers, and especially educating young people about being on the water and at sea. For me, there is nothing more enjoyable, and I am grateful for all that I have learned and experienced.

Below are just a few topics that a captain's license course will cover:

- Rules of the Road
- Radio Operations
- Survival Techniques
- Distress Signaling
- Boating Terminology
- Boat Equipment
- Use of Flares
- Techniques of Seamanship
- Anchoring
- Aides to Navigation
- Boat Registration and Documentation
- Marlinspike (Knot Tying)
- Use of Life Jackets
- Fire Fighting

"The Call of the Sea organization exposes kids and young people to the ocean, seamanship, and sailing."

Chapter 10

CALL OF THE SEA

The Call of the Sea (COTS) organization had been operating for more than eight years by the time I got involved with the group. It is such a wonderful educational/nonprofit organization that exposes kids and young people to the ocean, seamanship, and sailing. After making contact with Alan Olson in 2012, I slowly grew more interested in Call of the Sea and the idea of leaving a legacy with my experience that would help young people in the future.

Call
Sea

Two amigos, Alan and me, on the Matthew Turner, *February 29, 2020*

Many kids might be interested in learning more about sailing and the ocean, but they really have no idea until you get them out there on the water. Like me, some are so mesmerized by the whole thing and fall in love with the experience of sailing the ocean. Fortunately for me, my dad introduced me to boating and what it meant to be out on the water, exposing me to a lot of different fisherman and people of the sea. Once I was hooked on sailing and being out on the water, I found myself running with other like-minded people who shared my passion for the sea

The mission of Call of the Sea is to "provide inclusive and equitable access to on-the-water, science-based, educational programs that foster the connection to watersheds, ocean environments, and nautical heritage." Their vision is to "empower generations of students of all ages and backgrounds to become environmental stewards and transform their world through on-the-water field experiences."

Founded in 1985 by Alan Olson and a group of local sailors, COTS was formed to provide the youth of the Bay Area an opportunity to sail traditionally rigged sailing vessels and to learn about the marine environment and maritime history while inspiring them to become stewards of the sea.

In 2004, COTS received a boost with the help of Ken Neal along with a new group of committed sailors who came together to purchase the schooner *Seaward*. Over the past 10 years, *Seaward* has served over 50,000 students and now sails with an average of 5,000+ students every year.

Alan was instrumental in forming the organization's Educational Tall Ship in 2011. It took a while to get things up and running between design work and actually building a ship that would allow us to be involved in this type of education, taking people of all ages out on sailing boat trips. When I learned about the project, I was very excited about it and realized I could help out through donations and my commitment to the project in terms of fundraising. Alan expressed how grateful he is to me that when times were tough, I helped keep the organization going, and it has been a real pleasure to work with him on this endeavor.

In January of 2015, COTS merged with Educational Tall Ship, Inc. (ETS), the organization constructing the 132-foot wooden hybrid tall ship *Matthew Turner* in Sausalito, California. The ship also serves as a floating classroom for students, extending their capacity to serve the Northern California community and into Hawaii. For example, we take the Boy Scouts and Girl Scouts (14–18 years of age) down to Newport Beach for one week between Christmas and New Year's Day because they are out of school for that week. We also run a number of programs in Mexico and Puerto Vallarta exposing kids in that part of the world to sailing.

SAN FRANCISCO MARITIME

Crew handling the braces aboard the Matthew Turner

After six years of construction, Brigantine *Matthew Turner* is now transitioning from construction to full operation in order to perform its vital mission of educating young people in the Bay Area and beyond. In order to perform this mission, we had to get a Certificate of Inspection (COI) from the US Coast Guard, Marine Safety Division, to ensure that the *Matthew Turner* has the equipment, documentation, and crew to successfully operate the vessel.

Matthew Turner will inspire people to celebrate and experience the rich maritime history of the Bay Area, provide a platform to learn about and preserve our delicate ecosystem, and offer life-changing experiential learning opportunities for youth of all backgrounds, now and for generations to come.

Matthew Turner

Photos on pages 110-111 courtesy of Call of the Sea
(The three photos above ©San Francisco Maritime Library)

The first picture on the left shows Matthew Turner himself, who immigrated to the Bay Area from his home on Lake Erie in 1850. Getting into the gold industry proved successful, so he traveled back to the East Coast to purchase a ship to get into the shipping business for the booming lumber trade. His first ship he built was the *Nautilus*, in 1868, which outperformed all other ships at the time, raising the bar for sailing ship design. Known for his full aft, narrow fore hull design, he is considered the most prolific builder of sailing ships in history, with 228 vessels built by 1907. Moving the displacement of the ship aft, he was able to narrow the bow of the ship, creating a sleeker entry through the water, which gave his vessels more stability and speed, making for a better-sailing ship in all sea conditions.

Though Turner's legacy is impressive and worthy of reproduction, his designs would not satisfy our mission to provide environment education on a sailing educational tall ship that would represent the rich maritime history in the San Francisco Bay area. To connect the old with the new, Call of the Sea commissioned Tri-Coastal Marine to design a brand-new vessel based on Turner's original design that includes a relatively flat sheer, fine entry, straight run, and a little drag in the keel. The sailing ship mimics his traditional brigantine rig but complies with the US Coast Guard requirements for carrying passengers.

The safety requirements include watertight doors and bulkheads, a second regenerative power system for when there is no wind, and a twin steering design known as a "two screw" that allows the ship to be steered in ways other than the central steering wheel.

Call of the Sea installed numerous safety equipment as well as the latest navigation technology to ensure the tall ship can operate both locally and globally. It successfully passed its stability test in response to an ocean-going environment, and in the first quarter of 2020, the US Coast Guard tested the ship and crew for their response to a variety of emergencies including man overboard, fire, and flooding. We are all excited about the completion of the Brigantine *Matthew Turner* and putting it in full swing for the spring 2020 school field trip season.

Matthew Turner *ship build in progress (Bottom photo ©John Skoriak)*

Like me, Alan found life on the water was the best thing he could do with his life, including sailing his boat, the *Magellan*, around the world. Settling in the San Francisco Bay area suited him really well because he either owned a boat or was sailing on *Seaward*. When we first met and he learned of my love for sailing and star finding, he invited me on a schooner race, where I met several navigators. Alan and his wife have been huge supporters of Call of the Sea and have sailed all sorts of boats together over the years.

Working with Alan over the past few years has been a wonderful experience, with his "can-do" attitude, and I see no end to what we can accomplish through this amazing organization. It is a joy to work with all the volunteers and staff of Call of the Sea, an incredible group of talented individuals who share my passion for sailing and the sea.

> "*Mathew Turner* has been outfitted with safety equipment as well as the latest navigational technology to ensure the tall ship can operate both locally and globally."

Square sails raised for the first time on the Matthew Turner

Captain Adrian with Captain Terry and below Captain Alan aboard the Matthew Turner *sailing on the bay in San Francisco*

About the Author

GILL TERRY CAUSEY

A lifelong ocean-cruising sailor and a patron of maritime causes and projects from Hawaii (where he lived for more than half his life) to California, Terry Causey now divides his time between Kona, Hawaii, Sausalito, and Newport Beach, California. He holds his captain's license, endorsed for sailing all oceans, and has navigated throughout the Pacific, including the Hawaiian Islands, French Polynesia, New Zealand, Australia, and the Cook, Solomon, and Line Islands.

A successful real estate investor, Terry continues to be a significant benefactor to Call of the Sea. He believes in teaching young people stewardship of the oceans and instilling in them mindfulness of their environment and compassion for each other through education programs that foster a connection to the ocean and nautical heritage. He wants to empower generations of students of all ages and backgrounds to become environmental stewards and transform their world through on-the-water field experiences.

He is most proud of the Educational Tall Ship (ETS) that callofthesea.org constructed, the 132-foot wooden hybrid, propulsion system tall ship *Matthew Turner* in Sausalito, California. This ship will also serve as a floating classroom for students, extending the capacity to serve the Northern California community and beyond.

Gill Terry Causey and his dog, Akamai, in front of the Mathew Turner

For more information about

CALL OF THE SEA

please call (415) 331-3214

or email: info@callofthesea.org

Call of the Sea, 3020 Bridgeway #278, Sausalito, CA 94965

In Memoriam

World Circumnavigator Nancy Griffith

It was somewhere back in 1979, I believe and I had been in Kona for a year or so and I was itching to get out on the ocean. I read an ad in *West Hawaii Today* stating that "World Circumnavigator Nancy Griffith" was offering lessons in celestial navigation at Big Island Marine Store in the evening. I jumped at the chance because it sounded so interesting and adventurous. Thus we met and liked each other right off so when Nancy later offered blue water sailing lessons on board the *Nelly Bly*, I immediately signed up. She was a great teacher and fun to hang out with, so full of stories, and she had such a kind respect for everyone. She was so eager for all of her students to learn and become self-sufficient.

After that class she asked if I would help crew the *Nelly Bly* to Nawiliwili on Kauai. I, of course, jumped at that invitation, one for the experience but mainly because of the confidence Nancy gave to her crew to be able to accomplish any task set before them.

The trip to Kauai was wild, wet, and windy sailing across all the main channels through squalls and darkness but Nancy was so enthusiastic and joyful at being out in such dramatic elements that it was contagious.

That was my first sail through the islands in conditions I had never seen before but what a grand adventure Nancy took me on and thus began a great friendship with a wonderful lady.

Aloha, Terry